The Synagogue Through the Ages

A Jewish Refugee with the Torah—sculpture by Batya Leschinsky

Torah Shield, Prague, 1784

The Synagogue Through the Ages

by Azriel Eisenberg

BLOCH PUBLISHING COMPANY

New York

Library of Congress Catalog Card Number: 73–77284

ISBN: 0–8197–0291–9

Acknowledgments

The author and publisher acknowledge with thanks and appreciation the courtesies and permissions granted by the following institutions, publishers and individuals to reproduce the photographs in the book:

Ariel magazine, Jerusalem, Summer 1967	p. 39
Ariel magazine, Jerusalem, Autumn, 1967	p. 194 (top right; middle; bottom left and right)
Anabi, Tel Aviv	p. i
British Museum, London	p. 28
Cochin Synagogue: 400th Anniversary Souvenir Book by S. S. Koder	p. 73 (top)—p. 75
Committee on Jewish Chaplaincy: National Jewish Welfare Board	p. 188
Committee to Preserve the Ancient Synagogue of Sardis-Archaeological Exploration of Sardis	p. 58
Congregation Mikve Israel-Emanuel, Curaçao	p. 127 Foto Fischer (top) Synagogue Guide (Bottom)
David Kidouchim, Djerba, Tunisia	p. 80
Department of Torah Education and Culture of the World Zionist Organization	p. 198
Florence Synagogue Guide	p. 163 (top)
Forest Hills Jewish Center, New York	p. 182
Hebrew Union College—Jewish Institute of Religion	p. 73 (bottom)
Israel Ministry of Foreign Affairs, Jerusalem	p. 173
Israel Office of Information	Preface, p. 5, 12, 20, 32, 49, 53, 55, 58, 118 (bottom), 168, 170, 173, 191
Israel Government Tourist Office	p. 12 (bottom)
Jewish Encyclopedia, Funk and Wagnalls, N.Y.	p. 109 (top), 118 (top), 124, 163 (bottom)

Land of the Bible, American Fund for Israel Institutions	p. 71
Library of Congress	p. 131
Mittelalterliche Synagogen, Berlin, Richard Krautheimer	p. 143
Monumenta Judaica	p. 147, 194 (lower center)
New York Board of Rabbis	p. 184 (top)
Photographic Archives of the Jewish Theological Seminary of America, New York, by Frank J. Darmstaedter	p. 57,
Prague-Jewish Museum Frontispiece	p. ii, 95, 105
Solomon D. Sassoon; London	p. 83
Spanish Tourist Office	p. 97
Strasbourg Synagogue Dedication Book	p. 161
Synagoga: Recklinghausen	p. 193
Synagogale Altertümer by Samuel Kraus	p. 35, 63
Temple Beth Sholom, Elkins Park, Pennsylvania	p. 179
Temple Emanuel, New York City	p. 153
Torah: Illustrated Bible with German translation by Julius Furst	p. 15
United States Air Force Academy, Colorado Springs, Colorado	p. 184 (bottom)
The Yellow Star, Gerhard Schoenberner	p. 166 (right)
Wooden synagogues of Poland by Maria and Kazimierz, Warsaw, Poland	p. 115

The author and publisher acknowledge with thanks permissions to reprint from the following works:

B. Halper, *Post-Biblical Hebrew Literature*, Courtesy Jewish Publication Society, Philadelphia. Page 63 ff.

Sholem Asch, *Salvation*, Putnam; Copyright 1934, 1951, 1962 by Ruth Shaffer, Moses Asch, John Asch and the representative of Nathan Asch. All rights reserved. Page 122 f.

Naphtali Taylor Philips, *Unwritten History*, Courtesy American Jewish Archives, Cincinnati, Ohio. Page 133 f.

Herbert Samuel, *Memoirs*, Courtesy Curtis Brown, London. Page 172.

Quotations from *The Holy Scriptures*, Jewish Publication Society, Philadelphia.

With love to my brothers, sister and their spouses:
Leonard and Audree,
Irving and Esther,
Chana and Jesse Selter

Contents

Preface

The Synagogue Through the Ages is one of a series of introductory books for the study of Jewish institutions in which I have been engaged. Others now in print are *The Story of the Jewish Calendar, The Story of the Prayer Book* (in collaboration with Philip Arian) and *The Book of Books*. Several are in the process of publication and preparation.

I am indebted to Rabbi Max Arzt for a critical reading of the text; to Rabbi Ben-Zion Bokser, my dear friend and mentor, who suggested a number of improvements which were very helpful; and to the late Mrs. Max Lazare, who gave my efforts much encouragement. My wife, Rose, as always, read proof and helped in the index. Finally, I am beholden to the agencies, publishers and individuals who gave me permission to use the documentary illustrations and quotations.

Azriel Eisenberg

Ancient stone menorah found in Tiberias, third century

The Synagogue Through the Ages

I
Biblical Origins

Writing of the synagogue, the noted Christian scholar R. T. Herford said: "No human institution has a longer unbroken history, and none has done more for uplifting the human race."* The synagogue existed hundreds of years before the Christian church was founded; it preceded by more than a thousand years the mosque, the Moslem house of worship. Precisely where and when it had its beginning no one can really say. The quest for the origin of the synagogue is somewhat like tracing to its source a mighty river whose headwaters originate high in the mountains and are fed by lakes and streams.

Let us briefly trace its historic and religious background, beginning with the source of all sources, the Bible. As a matter of fact, the Bible contains no mention of the synagogue. The word would have puzzled the ancient Hebrews; it is derived from the Greek word *synagoge* which means "gathering" or "assembly." A Hebrew phrase that we do find frequently in Exodus (e.g., Ex. 29:42–44; 30:19–20, etc.) and that more closely approximates the meaning of this Greek term is *Ohel Moed*, or "tent of meeting," which will be touched upon on page 7.

From its very beginning in the book of Genesis to the end in Chronicles, the Bible is a record of man seeking God. Repelled by man-made idols and their worship, Abraham glimpsed a vision of One God, Ruler of the Universe. Isaac, Jacob and their descendants brooded on the God of Abraham and experienced many encounters

*Quoted by Joseph H. Hertz, *The Authorised Daily Prayer Book*, New York, Bloch Pub., 1948, p. xvii.

3

with Him. Moses came upon Him at the Burning Bush. In Exodus, Chapter 3, we read of Moses' surprise encounter with the ancestral God while tending a flock of sheep on the mountain of God. There an angel appeared before him in a flame of fire in the midst of a burning bush. Although the entire bush was aflame, the fire did not consume it. And Moses said: *I must turn aside now to look at this wondrous sight, why the bush is not burnt.* And when the Lord saw that he turned aside to see, God called unto him and said: *Moses, Moses.* And Moses said: *Here am I.* And He said: *Do not come closer. Remove your sandals from your feet, for the place on which you stand is holy ground.* The communication that follows between God and Moses is in the form of a dialogue which is the language of worship in the synagogue; and the place where He makes Himself known is sacred. In Moslem lands no one may enter a mosque without first taking off his shoes. Oriental Jews also remove their shoes when entering a synagogue.

This first solemn engagement between God and Moses was the harbinger of Jewish peoplehood and Jewish life. From it flowed the ceaseless preoccupation of the Children of Israel with the questions: Where may one find God? Is His Presence limited to a specific place? How does He communicate with man? How shall we serve Him?

The Covenant at Sinai

This extraordinary experience was the turning point in Moses' life and in the life of the Jewish people. It was the opening scene of the great drama of their delivery from the bondage of Egypt. As Moses led his people through the trackless wastes of the desert, he prepared them for the great drama of the Revelation at Mount Sinai. How the Ten Commandments were given to the Hebrews is told in Chapter 20, the most important of the Book of Exodus:

> And the Lord called Moses to the top of the mount which trembled greatly and Moses went up . . . And God spoke these words [in Hebrew they are called the "Ten Words"] saying: I am the Lord your God, who brought you out of the land of Egypt, out of the house of bondage. You shall have no other gods before Me.

This, of course, was the first of the Ten Commandments that were

Mount Sinai (Jebel Musa), Sinai Desert. In the foreground is the Saint Catherine Monastery

Ancient Israelite Sanctuary, excavated at Arad, Negev

to become the foundation of Judaism. But there was much more. Immediately following the Ten Words, God instructed Moses to say to the people (Chapter 20:19-23):

> You yourselves have seen that I have talked with you from heaven . . . An altar of earth you shall make for Me, and shall sacrifice your burnt-offerings . . . In every place where I cause My Name to be mentioned I will come to you and bless you.

And the teaching continues:

> And if you make Me an altar of stones you shall not build it of hewn [or dressed] stones for if you lift up your tool [i.e., a metal instrument] upon it, you will have profaned [the altar].

These were very significant statements indeed, pregnant with meaning, as will be explained below.

Prophetic Ideas

In these teachings we glimpse the nub of the message voiced by the prophets. God needs no intermediary to speak with the people. His Divine Presence is not confined to one place. The specific place which becomes holy by the "mention of His Name" need not be a dazzling and glamorous structure. Above all, firmly attached to the place of His worship is one other idea: peace. Metal tools are not to be used in building His sanctuary because they are instruments of war and destruction.

As is known, the idea of sacrifice was common throughout the ancient world. The temples of Greece and other pagan countries invariably contained an altar where rites of sacrifice took place. The dictionary defines the word *sacrifice* as coming from two Latin words: *sacer* for "sacred," and *ficare* "to make" (an offering to a deity). Since so many people in those days were herdsmen, the sacrifice often consisted of killing and burning a choice animal selected from a herd of cattle or sheep. The Hebrew word for sacrifice, however, reflects a radically different idea. It is *korban*, derived from the root which means "coming near." The essence of Jewish worship is to draw near to the Divine spiritually, emotionally and intellectually.

But as we shall see, these ideas were too advanced for the early Israelites. It took many years for these basic teachings of the prophets to penetrate. Surrounded by peoples who paid homage to idols and worshiped supernatural beings, they absorbed ideas foreign to Judaism.

God's Dwelling Place

In their forty years of wandering the Israelites were sustained by faith in God's divine guidance. Little by little the rabble began to understand and experience the deeper meaning of their being and their destiny. They began to feel that they were becoming a "community," bound to the God of Abraham and to each other. Moses repeatedly exhorted them to hearken to the words of the Lord, as expressed in Exodus, Chapter 19: *If you will obey My voice and keep My covenant, you shall be My own possession among all peoples, for all the earth is Mine, and you shall be a kingdom of priests and a holy nation.* Although the people answered immediately, *All that the Lord has spoken we will do,* it nevertheless took them many, many years to learn what it meant to be a people of the Covenant.

While Moses was on Mount Sinai, he was instructed to erect a Tabernacle, furnish it and prescribe the order of its service. Several chapters in Exodus (35-40) are devoted to the story of the Tabernacle. In Hebrew the word is *Mishkan,* which means "dwelling place." It was also the "tent of meeting" for God and Moses and the people. In the regulations governing its construction the idea of "sacrifice" was still further extended. We read in Chapter 25:

> And the Lord spoke unto Moses saying: Speak unto the children of Israel, that they bring Me a gift offering; you shall accept gifts for Me from every person whose heart so moves him and makes him willing . . . gold, silver, and copper. . . and fine linen . . . and rams' skins dyed red . . . , and acacia-wood; oil for the lighting, spices for the anointing oil, and for the sweet incense . . . And let them make Me a sanctuary, that I may dwell among them . . . They shall make an ark of acacia-wood . . . and you shall overlay it with pure gold . . . And you shall put into the ark the testimony which I shall give you . . .

The above shows that offerings to God were to be gifts other than burnt animals or sweet incense. Moreover, they were to be offered voluntarily, without being compelled, *by every man whose heart makes him willing* to give.

Anyone familiar with the synagogue knows that its central feature is the Holy Ark, the *Aron Kodesh*. The word *aron* in Hebrew means a box or chest. (The Sephardim* call it *hekhal*.) The testimony it contained was none other than the two tablets of stone that Moses had brought down from Mount Sinai, on which were engraved the Ten Commandments. The building of the Ark was carefully directed by divine command; it became one of the most precious possessions of the Jewish people. Until the holy Temple was erected, it was in portable form leading the people on their journeys in the desert and in battle. It was given a permanent resting place only when Solomon built the Temple in Jerusalem.

The *mishkan* housed a number of sacred objects which are mentioned in the chapter on Solomon's Temple. One of these was the *ner tamid*, the eternal lamp (Exodus 27:20). Light has always accompanied the service of the Lord. An aphorism popular in Judaism claims that "the lamp of God is the soul of man." The sobriquet "lamp" or "light" was used as an honorary title, e.g., Rabbenu Gershom, the Light of the Diaspora (965-1025). And as you remember, the creation began with the divine command, "Let there be light."

Another sacred fixture was the menorah. The specifications for its construction are found in Exodus 25:31-39, 38:17-24. It became one of the most popular symbols in the Jewish heritage. Flanked by two olive branches, it is the emblem of the State of Israel.

The Priests (Cohanim) and the Levites

Employed in the service of the Tabernacle were the Priests and Levites. The former were chiefly responsible for conducting the sacrificial offerings and serving as religious teachers, while the Levites were entrusted with the tasks connected with the Tabernacle. The title of the Book of Leviticus, which follows Exodus, is derived from the name of Levi, whose descendants subsequently constituted one of the twelve tribes of Israel. Moses and his brother Aaron were

*Jews from the Mediterranean countries.

Levites. From the family of Aaron came the Priests; from Moses the Levites. The entire Book of Leviticus, *Vayikra*, and part of the Book of Numbers, *Bamidbar*, explain the duties of the priests and Levites in great detail.

In Numbers, beginning with the end of Chapter 1, we learn a good deal about their duties, their services and the sources of their livelihood. They possessed "no inheritance in the land." They were given tithes and certain other payments and offerings. *I give you the priesthood as a service or gift*, said the Lord to Aaron (18:7). Further on we read: *I am thy portion and thine inheritance among the children of Israel (18:20).*

These laws may have been instituted to make the Priests and Levites dependent on the people, thus preventing them from acquiring political power and ruling over them, as was the case in Egypt, Babylonia and other countries near them.

The Priesthood, including that of the Levites, was hereditary. Although the Jewish people have had no active priesthood since the destruction of the Temple in 70 C.E., the tradition of the priestly line is still commemorated in the synagogue and in certain Jewish observances. Even today, the honor of being called up first for the reading of the Torah in the synagogue is given to Cohanim, descendants of Aaron the priest, and to Levites, who are next to be called up. After them come the Israelites, comprising the majority not descended from the tribe of Levi. There are other prestigious functions at which these honored few officiate, such as blessing the congregation at the conclusion of the synagogue service—a practice observed by traditional congregations—and serving as religious functionaries in the redemption of the firstborn son. They are also subject to strict laws prohibiting their contamination and regulating their choice of a wife. All of this and more may be found in books on Jewish laws and observances.

Intrinsic to the story of the synagogue, therefore, are the fundamental prophetic ideas promulgated in the Bible, as follows: 1) God is universal; 2) He may be served by the heart's yearning to be near Him; 3) He may be approached directly without intermediaries; 4) His servants (in early times they were the Priests and Levites) must be pure and dedicated. These are the very foundations of the synagogue. These lessons were intensified and brought home again and again as the Children of Israel settled in the Promised Land.

II

Trial and Triumph

The Promised Land

Those well-known forty years of wandering in the desert were years of refining, indoctrinating and preparing for the challenges ahead in the practical reality of settling the Promised Land. The exodus from Egypt, the land of slavery, was a relief. The experiences in the desert were novel. The former slaves were exhilarated by their victories, by the wondrous events that transpired at the Red Sea and at Mount Sinai, and by their increasing awareness of having been chosen as a people marked by God. Seas of sand surrounded them. They were alone and isolated. There were no distractions or temptations. And their contacts with their leaders, Moses, Aaron and Joshua, were direct and frequent.

Then came the great moment of realization, the climax of forty years of preparation and anticipation. On a day early in spring, about 1250 B.C.E., the twelve tribes of Israel, led by Joshua, crossed the Jordan River into the Promised Land. The Ark of the Covenant was borne at the head of the invasion into Canaan. As a rule, in the spring of the year, when the winter snows melt high on the slopes of Mount Hermon, the Jordan overflows. But this time it was different, and the miracle of a dry river bed helped in the crossing. Surely this was the finger of God. It strengthened their faith; morale was high.

The ancient city of Jericho was the first target of attack. We read in Joshua (Chapter 6) of the strange siege, the Israelites' circling around the walls, heartened by the presence of the Ark in their

midst, accompanied by seven priests blowing seven rams' horns.
Soon the walls came tumbling down.

Canaan, at the time of the invasion, was a rich plum ripe for the
picking. Ruled by petty kings of small city-states, it was very vulnera-
ble. The Canaanites, divided geographically by hills and valleys,
were disunited. Mighty Egypt, which had kept a firm rule, was now
weakened. The Hebrew invaders were united, strong in their belief
in the God of the Fathers and inspired by confidence in their destiny
and the conquest of the land promised them. They carried the day,
subduing local chiefs and conquering one city-state after another.

In the Book of Judges, where the conquest is graphically described, we read again and again as in a refrain: *The Israelites did evil
in the sight of the Lord . . . So He handed them over into the power
of . . . And the Israelites cried to the Lord . . . And the Lord raised
a deliverer . . .* and so on.

Evidently, the change from nomadic to city living and from
being shepherds to farmers was quite difficult. In giving up their
wandering style of life and adapting to conditions in permanently
settled areas, and in learning to till the soil and plant vineyards and
olive trees, they leaned heavily on their neighbors. The religion of
the Canaanites was intimately related to the phenomena of nature.
The cycle of planting, growth and harvest was conceived and
enacted as the drama of human birth and death. Birth in nature was
equated with the process of sexual intercourse, with alluring goddesses and seductive rites of mating symbolizing fertility and growth.
The rites were erotic and involved sacred prostitution. When a blight
or drought struck the land, the gods of nature had to be appeased,
even by the sacrifice of children. Baal and Ashtarot were the supreme male and female gods, who headed a host of lesser gods and
goddesses. They were the "masters" of the fields, vineyards, trees—
indeed of all nature. They were worshiped by various pagan practices and had to be placated for man's trespassing on their domains.
The Canaanite religion was a complex chaos of superstitions and
fears which appealed to the primitive mind. This pagan worship was,
as the Hebrews well knew, "evil in the sight of the Lord." Yet it
penetrated the lives of the Israelites—from high placed rulers to the
lowly peasants. Even King Saul and King David gave their children
names ending with *baal.* In the early period of Jewish history the
Israelites often worshiped both the God of Abraham and the baal

Temple Mount, Site of First and Second Temple, Jerusalem. The Dome is the Mosque of Omar.

Rachel's Tomb, Bethlehem

gods without sensing any conflict between them. Even the "good" people may have believed that the God of the Covenant was the Lord of the spirit, and Baal the lord of the fertility of the soil who provided the cycles of rain and sun and made the fields, vineyards and olive groves fruitful.

Israel's prophets and spiritual leaders insisted that there was but one God and none other. There could be no compromise, no "togetherness." Again and again the people were chastised. Joshua, for example, at the Assembly at Shechem (Chapter 24) after rehearsing Israel's history, demanded, *Choose this day whom you will serve.* This impassioned plea was reiterated in successive generations by judges and prophets.

The Tabernacle and Holy Ark

The focus where this conflict centered was, of course, the *Mishkan* (Tabernacle) and the *Aron Kodesh* (Holy Ark). As stated in the preceding chapter, the Tabernacle, God's sanctuary, may also have served as the tent of meeting. As the invading Israelites conquered the central highlands, the Tabernacle moved with them. Finally it found a resting place at Shiloh, where it stayed until the Philistines wrested the Ark from them and took it into captivity. The Philistines were a warlike people who had invaded Canaan from the islands west of the mainland. "Sea peoples" was what the Egyptians called them. The name Palestine comes from this people who challenged the invasion of the tribes from the desert. They initiated the use of iron weapons. Against these the primitive weapons of the Israelites were as effective as bows and arrows are against rifles today. When the Philistines defeated the Israelites the people cried, *Why has the Lord smitten us? Let us fetch the Ark from Shiloh that He may come among us and rescue us.* When the Ark was brought into the camp, all Israel raised a mighty shout, so that the earth rang. Hearing it the Philistines asked, *What means this mighty shout in the camp of the Hebrews?* When they learned that the Ark of the Lord had come into the camp, they wailed, Woe unto us!. . . *Who shall deliver us out of the power of these mighty gods?* The fame of the Ark was such that their faith in the invincibility of their own weapons vanished. From this story it is quite evident that the Ark was looked upon as a cult object, possessing supernatural powers.

But the warlike Philistines gathered up their courage and waged a great battle near the site of present-day Tel Aviv. This time, even the Ark did not prevent the Israelites' defeat. What happened must have come as an almost unimaginable calamity. The Ark was taken by the Philistines; and Hophni and Phineas, the two sons of the High Priest Eli, who accompanied it on its journeyings, were slain. The supernatural symbols of the Ark were shattered.

The despair and panic into which the Israelites were plunged, the wanderings of the Ark for seven months, the plagues that befell the Philistines, and the Ark's final return are told in I Samuel, Chapters 4-6. Now the Israelites set it up at Kiriath-Yearim, in the central highlands. Jerusalem, ultimately the final home of the Ark, was only about ten miles away. However, many years would elapse before its arrival there.

The conflicts between the prophets and the people, including their leaders, judges, kings and queens, continued for many years and are described in the books of Judges, Samuel and Kings. The most dramatic of these is the vivid and stirring episode of Elijah's struggle against Ahab and Jezebel and his contest with the priest of Baal on Mount Carmel. His name marked him (*Eli*, my God, is *Yah*) as the most outstanding spiritual leader of the time. The vacillation between God and Baal during those formative years of the Jewish people are epitomized in Elijah's challenge: *How long will you be hopping around from one to the other? If Yahweh is God, follow Him, but if baal—follow him!*

While the religions of the peoples of Canaan had a great deal in common, Israel's religion was unique. Like oil and water it would not mix or blend. God was alone, sovereign of the universe, ruler of every aspect of nature and life, demanding full obedience to his law. He could not be influenced or controlled by magic, sorcery, sex rites and the like. And He would not tolerate any other deities beside Him.

It took many generations of struggle to overcome the worship of Baal and Ashtarot and to destroy the *bamot* (high places), the sacred trees and variety of cult objects. The tribes strayed often but were not swallowed up by the nations around them. Their covenant with God helped them remain an *Am Segulah* (a chosen people), distinct and set apart. They had acquired an enduring "inner voice" which moved them to turn to the Lord when in anguish. When they lost the "glory of Israel," i.e. the Holy Ark, to the Philistines, it did not down them. Their resilience was not reduced nor their vitality weakened. When Shiloh declined, a new home was found. God's Covenant was a living thing, not dependent on any one place. Its promise sustained their confidence and trust in the God of Abraham.

Tabernacle utensils and ornaments of the High Priest

III

Solomon's Temple

Jerusalem

At the time Shiloh was destroyed, Jerusalem was the stronghold of the Jebusites, a Canaanite tribe. About thirty years later, Saul became the first king of Israel. David, his successor, reigned from around 1000 to 965 B.C.E. He swept the Philistines out of the land and contained them in three coastal cities. He reunited Israel and extended its borders, bringing under his control Syria and the lands to the east extending almost to the Euphrates River. Capturing Jerusalem from the Jebusites, he established it as the capital of the Israelite kingdom.

Although David brought the Ark to Jerusalem from Kiriath-Yearim, he was never to see the splendid sanctuary built to house it permanently. But he did acquire the site on which the Temple was to be erected. And he made thorough preparations for his son Solomon to build it.

The poignant story as to why David was not found worthy to build the Temple is told in II Samuel, Chapter 7. It contains overtones alluding to the very meaning of the Temple. These are emphasized in the scriptural story. After David had rested from fighting his enemies around about, he remarked sadly to Nathan the prophet: *See now I dwell in a house of cedar but the Ark of God dwells within curtains.* That night the word of the Lord came to Nathan instructing him to tell King David, *When your days are fulfilled . . . I will establish your son's kingdom. He shall build a house for my name.* David did not merit building a permanent house to the Lord because he had been a warrior and had shed much blood (I Chronicles, 22:8).

Solomon's Temple

In the fourth year of his reign, having obtained the assistance of Hiram of Tyre and a multitude of Phoenician workmen, Solomon commenced the huge task. As with the altar, no hammer, axe or other tools of iron were employed in the actual construction because iron is used for weapons of war and the Temple was to be a symbol of peace. The Temple was built of large blocks of stone from the Jerusalem quarries (some still carry Solomon's name) and cedarwood imported from Lebanon. The site of the Temple was in the center of Mount Moriah in the southern quarter of Jerusalem. Although no trace of the Temple is extant (since at present the site is occupied by a Moslem mosque), we know the facts from the Bible story. Basically, it was modeled after the Tabernacle but was about double in size. Intended as a permanent sanctuary, it contained chambers for the Priests and Levites and for the Temple treasures and stores. Oriented east to west, it consisted of three sections: a hall *(Ulam)*, a shrine *(Hekhal)* and the Holy of Holies *(Devir)* measuring altogether 113¾ × 32½ feet. Fronting the building was a portico with two imposing bronze columns, nearly 30 feet high, which were named *Yachin* (He will establish) and *Boaz* (in strength). In the hall was a large basin for the Priests to wash and cleanse themselves and a large metal altar. Worship took place in the shrine which led off from the hall. It held the altar of incense and the Table of Showbread with fine gold candlesticks standing on each side. Its windows were narrow without and wider within. Leading off from the shrine was the Holy of Holies, which was shaped like a perfect cube and built on a higher level. Lined with cedar and overlaid with pure gold, it contained the Holy Ark which was adorned with two *cherubim* made of olive wood and gold. It was windowless and shrouded in a continuous, awesome stillness.

The Temple was surrounded by a three-story structure which contained rooms and cells for storing the Temple vessels and treasures. It was part of a complex of buildings which included the King's palace, a palace for Solomon's chief wife (Pharaoh's daughter), the throne room and administrative offices. These were built on lower terraces of the hill. What an impressive dazzling sight they must have been against the grey and brown rocks of the hills of Jerusalem!

The dedication of the Temple during the *Feast of Sukkot* was an

Moslems praying in a mosque

Deuteronomy. Josiah summóned the people to hear it read aloud on a day during Passover in 621 B.C.E. We can visualize how they must have listened for the first time in their lives to the *Shema:*

> *Hear, O Israel, the Lord is our God, the Lord is One. You shall love the Lord your God with all your heart.* . . . (Deuteronomy, 6:4–9)

They surely heard as well the law forbidding all sacrificial worship offerings, tithes and gifts, except in the Temple at Jerusalem, the seat of His presence. Josiah read the Book which was discovered in the profaned Temple and renewed the ancient Covenant that had been all but forgotten. This was no empty ceremony or perfunctory royal gesture; it was genuine. Country-wide reform followed and was pursued zealously and thoroughly. Baal worship and all the idolatrous cults, rites and "sacred" objects were abolished and destroyed. Sorcery, witchcraft, the "high places" and sanctuaries were broken up, their priests scattered and banished. In these reforms Josiah reached beyond his kingdom into the northern territories of Israel. The Jerusalem Temple was restored as the center of the Jewish life. The long-neglected Passover celebration was renewed and the people resumed their festival pilgrimages to Jerusalem, City of David, the religious and national capital. Josiah's reforms made an indelible impression on the historical consciousness of the Jewish people.

Bringing the Word of God to the People: Synagogue Origins

The "see-saw" between the worship of God and Baal was proof of how deeply felt at the time was the people's need for outlets of religious expression. The belief in and worship of divine guidance and care was innate in the lives of our ancestors. At the same time it also indicates that they felt certain inadequacies in the organized worship of the true God. No matter where His shrine was located, access to it was limited. Pilgrimages to the Holy City were difficult. The distance to Jerusalem was too far for those who lived in the north or south. Travel facilities were bad. Taking time off from tending the fields, olive groves and vineyards during the busy harvest and gleaning seasons was not only inconvenient but also risky. It was necessary, therefore, to bring the message of God to the people where they lived. These circumstances may account for what we read in II Chronicles (17:9) that during the reign of Jehoshaphat, who was king of Judea (while Ahab ruled the northern kingdom of Israel), the Levites *went about through all the cities of Judea and taught among the people.* Some scholars consider this a possible clue to the beginning of the synagogue as an institution. We find no record, it is true, of a special building where the Levites taught. But, as is natural in a dry, sunny climate, it is likely that the Israelites were in the habit of assembling in the open. Such gatherings are mentioned again and again throughout the Bible.

In the Book of Leviticus (23:2, 4, 27, etc.) for example, we find repeatedly the words *mikraei kodesh,* or "holy convocations." Does this mean that from very early times they held religious services other than those involving sacrifice? In II Kings, Chapter 4 there is an interesting story about a Shunamite woman who accommodated the prophet Elisha when he visited her hamlet. One day, finding her only child dead, she tells her husband that she must hurry to the "man of God" and ask him to revive the boy. Her husband replies: *"Why go to him today? It is neither the festival of the new moon nor the Sabbath day,* implying that she will not find him except on these days. Such visits, it is suggested, would not have been social calls; they must have been gatherings for worship. Shall we infer from this conversation that it was the custom to visit the prophet on certain special days?

Is it not reasonable to assume from the above and from Solomon's dedicatory address that some form of public worship besides animal sacrifices was already then known to the Children of Israel?

Further, during the reign of the backsliding kings, as we have seen, the Temple was polluted by the worship of other gods. The prophets of the true God must have held meetings with their followers. Where? We do not know where the meetings took place but it seems certain that take place they did, secretly. Otherwise no reform could have been possible under King Josiah's rule.

The proponent of these theories, Dr. Louis Finkelstein, noted scholar and long-time Chancellor of the Jewish Theological Seminary of America, concludes that "the Judeans of the seventh century B.C.E. could not have satisfied their religious wants with the three pilgrimages a year to Jerusalem prescribed in Deuteronomy. What was the peasant whose child was suddenly taken ill to do in order to obtain Divine mercy and forgiveness? . . . In an age when religion absorbed almost all the emotional life of man, the concentration of the worship of a whole country in a single edifice, no matter how beautiful and inspiring, must have been impossible."*

While most scholars believe, as will be shown in the coming chapter, that the synagogue originated in Babylonia, some maintain that it began in the days of the First Temple. Since there are no historical or archeological records to prove their argument, they base their theories on Biblical allusions. Thus Jeremiah, describing the capture of Jerusalem by Babylon, writes in Chapter 39:8: *And the Chaldeans burned down the royal palace and the house of the common people [bet-am].* The term *bet-am* for synagogue had been popular until the Rabbis forbade its use because it vulgarized the institution of the synagogue. Accordingly some scholars propose that synagogues did in fact exist in Judea before the Babylonian Exile.

A much more specific allusion is found in Psalm 74:7, 8 which is alleged to have been composed in the early period of the Babylonian Exile. It reads: *They [the enemy] have set Thy sanctuary on fire, they have laid it low and profaned Thy dwelling . . . They have burned up all the meeting-places of God in the land.* This statement is perhaps the most significant in dating the existence of some type of synagogue institution to the latter days of the First Temple.

We must keep in mind that three basic aims describe the origins of the institution known as the synagogue: 1) regular congregational worship; 2) reading of the Scriptures (i.e., selections from the Five Books of Moses as well as from the Prophets); 3) commenting on the portion read, or what may be described loosely as the delivery of a sermon. To apply these criteria to the theory of "the holy convocation" submitted above, we must make several assumptions. For example, we are not certain whether the gatherings were held daily or only on the Sabbath, New Moon and Festival Days. Nor are we certain that the people joined the leader in prayer. Moreover, since there probably were no scrolls for reading, it is quite possible that the prophets quoted the Scriptures from memory. And it is more than likely that their "sermons" were their own prophetic utterances, the very ones which have come down to us in writing. These presumed

*The Origin of the Synagogue, Proceedings, American Academy for Jewish Research, 1928–1930.

practices may fulfill the criteria stated above, suggesting the existence of a primitive kind of synagogue as far back as in the days of the First Temple.

King Josiah's reign was a decisive turning point. But were his reforms so radical as to forbid prayer worship everywhere except at the Temple? Some Biblical historians are persuaded that he was mindful of the needs of the Israelites who lived far from Jerusalem and could not join the pilgrimages to the Holy City as enjoined by the Scriptures. As he was religiously motivated, it is surmised that he permitted the practice of worship at the *bamot*, open sacred places, but without sacrifice. It seems inconceivable, they argue, that during the three pilgrimage festivals when many went up to the Holy City, those who remained behind had no place where they might go to give expression to their inner spiritual feelings. It may be, therefore, that the habit of regular worship without sacrifice, which characterizes the synagogue, began to be inculcated at this time, i.e., the sixth century B.C.E.

Evidences of chants of adoration and thanksgiving to God which may have been used at such services as well as in the Temple are found in Psalms 136, where the refrain *For His mercy endures forever* is repeated. It may have been a chant in which the Priests and worshipers participated. What is interesting to note is that this psalm, recounting God's goodness to Israel, ends with the Israelites' settlement in Canaan. This may be evidence of its origin in the period of the First Temple.

If these theories are correct, then the exiles in Babylonia carried on a tradition already established in the homeland. Whether they originated or continued the institution is a matter of opinion, but with the passing of time, the existence of the synagogue becomes more and more manifest through literary records and archeological evidences, as will be discussed in Chapter IV.

IV

The Synagogue Is Born

Fall of Israel

Events in the eighth century B.C.E. moved with inexorable speed. The kingdoms of Israel and Judea went through an agonizing, short-lived series of political alliances with their neighbors in an effort to halt the aggressive war machines of the giant empires to the east: ruthless and powerful Assyria and later Babylonia. Doom was, however, inescapable.

In 722 B.C.E. the northern kingdom of Israel came to an end. To make sure that its inhabitants would not rebel, a large number of Israelites were transported far to the east (Sargon deported 27,290 in 719) and replaced by conquered peoples from other countries. Those who remained behind intermarried with the transplanted settlers; their descendants were no longer known as Israelites but as Samaritans.

The kingdom of Judea lasted a few generations longer, on borrowed time. After the fall of Samaria, came the turn of Judea, situated in the south. Like their peers in the north, the kings of Judea had been trying to placate the Assyrians with tribute. There is an account in II Kings, Chapter 16, of how the Judean king Ahaz (735–715 B.C.E.) gave away some of the precious ornaments of the Temple to appease the enemy. Indeed, so terrified was he that, to pacify the angry gods, he even condemned his son to the flames as a sacrificial offering in the Valley of Hinnom in Jerusalem. (Because of these horrible practices this valley, *Gei Hinnom*, became a Hebrew term for hell.) In desperation, his successor, Hezekiah (727–698 B.C.E.), called on the

25

prophet Isaiah for guidance. He was directed to stop succumbing to the Assyrians, but to stand up to them instead. The result was that although Jerusalem found itself under siege, it did not fall. The Assyrian armies that surrounded it decided for some unknown reason to withdraw. (Some believe it was because of a plague.) To the astonished people of Jerusalem, this turn of events seemed a miracle. It took place in the spring of the year (714 B.C.E.) and Hezekiah forthwith proclaimed the celebration of Passover. According to II Chronicles, Chapter 30, there had not been the like since the time of Solomon.

But the power of Assyria was on the decline; it had given way to a new conqueror to the east, the Babylonian empire. This development may have accounted for the above miracle. Jerusalem had been spared, but only for a while. Now Judea entered a period of terror and political maneuvers to keep its independence. After the death of Hezekiah, Judea's political history became intertwined again with the surrounding countries; its religious practices degenerated. The long reign of Hezekiah's son, Manasseh, was abominable. So too was the short reign of the grandson who was assassinated. And then came Josiah (637 B.C.E.), whose extraordinary reforms we narrated in Chapter III. (It may be added here that luck was on Josiah's side. His reign occurred during the defeat of Assyria, resulting in a vacuum created by its collapse before the rise of Babylonia.) Then, in 586 B.C.E., the inevitable blow fell.

The First Exile

As the Babylonian armies swept toward Jerusalem, the city swarmed with refugees. Food supplies grew short and epidemics raged as its walls once again fell under siege. In the hot month of Tammuz in the year 586 B.C.E., the armies of the Babylonian conqueror Nebuchadnezzar breached the fortifications. A massacre ensued. King Zedekiah's eyes were put out. His sons were killed, as were the high priest and other members of the nobility. On the ninth day of Av the Temple itself was destroyed, and the people of Judea, like those of Israel before them, were forced into exile.

To this day, Jews are stirred anew by the horror and grief of that tragedy. Lines from Lamentations, whose authorship tradition ascribes to Jeremiah, are recited on Tisha B'Av by Jews sitting on the floor in dimly lit synagogues throughout the world:

How lonely is the city that was once full of people . . . She now sits like a widow . . . Judah has been banished into exile . . . Zion's gates are desolate; her priests despair. Her maidens have been carried away—bitter is her lot. (Lamentations, Ch.1)

The sorrow of the exiles is likewise the theme of Psalm 137.This lament, recited on week days before the grace after meals, is another reminder of that catastrophe:

> By the rivers of Babylon we sat down and wept
> When we remembered Zion . . .
> If I forget you O Jerusalem
> Let my right hand wither!
> Let my tongue stick to the roof of my mouth
> If I do not remember you,
> If I do not put Jerusalem
> Above my highest joy!

Ezekiel, the Prophet of Exile

It was the pledge never to forget Jerusalem that kept the exiles together. Their sense of belonging to a distinctive community was intensified. The knowledge that theirs was a shared history and tradition was a strong and living force. Despite the overwhelming national disaster the exiles remembered their oath; otherwise they would eventually have been absorbed into the life around them. This had in fact already happened to the exiles from the northern kingdom. Had it happened to the Judean exiles as well, the history of the Jews might well have ended by the waters of Babylon.

But it did not end there. For those exiles did not brood on past calamities but dwelled on the deliverance that had always followed. Their stubborn hope in the midst of despair was given expression by a prophet named Ezekiel, the first great leader of the Babylonian exiles. He was a priest who had been taken captive and brought to Babylon eleven years before the destruction of Jerusalem. Now, far from the Temple where he had served, *the word of the Lord came expressly unto Ezekiel . . . and the hand of the Lord was upon him.* His words brought hope and healing to his suffering brothers. His vision of the Valley of the Dead Bones so vividly described in Chapter 37 of Ezekiel, symbolizes the deliverance that would one day come. Evoked countless times by the Jewish people on their arduous journey through history, it has in reality been fulfilled many times over.

Such was the inflexible faith that kept the exiles together, and such the hope that one day they or their children would go home again to rebuild the land and the Temple that had been destroyed.

Meanwhile, what could replace the Temple in their exile? The great religious reforms of King Josiah were fresh in their minds; there was no thought of violating them. The Temple must remain the one place of worship. But until it could be rebuilt, worship must take other forms. Although we do not know precisely what those forms were, there are clues throughout the Book of Ezekiel. For example, Ezekiel, seated in his house with the elders of Judah sitting before him narrates that *the hand of the Lord God fell there upon me.* Again, in Ezekiel 14:1, we find the statement: *Then came certain of the elders of Israel to me, and sat before me;* and yet again, in Ezekiel 20:1. *In the seventh year, in the fifth month, on the tenth day of the month, certain of the elders of Israel came to inquire of the Lord, and sat before me.*

From all this, scholars have surmised that the home of Ezekiel had become a center for "inquiring of the Lord." The gatherings

The Cyrus Cylinder describing his victory over Babylonia

there must have been solemn ones, dedicated to recalling the nostalgic memories of the life they had left behind, and the heritage they shared. They must also have been times of self-examination, more thoughtful and soul-searching than ever before in their history.

One idea that emerged from their deliberations seemed altogether new. This was the idea that each individual is personally responsible for what he does. Although in our own lives today we often try to find someone or something to blame when things go wrong, we know that we ourselves are the guilty ones. The exiles were no different. But they had behind them a long tradition that went back to Moses and the Ten Commandments. According to Exodus 20:5, *I, the Lord your God am a zealous God, visiting the sins of the father upon the children to the third and the fourth generation of those who hate me* . . . Although this must have been intended as a warning against doing wrong, it could have been turned into an excuse for punishing the children of the guilty. Could that be right or just? Long before Ezekiel, thoughtful men among the Israelites had been troubled by seeing such things happen. In the graphic words of Ezekiel: *The fathers have eaten sour grapes, and the children's teeth are gritty* (18:2). In that case, what chance was there for the return of the children of the exiled to their homeland?

It remained for the prophet of the exiles, far from Jerusalem, to consider the problem at length and to set down his conclusions. They sound rather like a dialogue, and it is not hard to imagine that they grew out of much thoughtful reflection and discussion perhaps in his home between him and his audience:

> You ask, why should not children suffer for their parents' sins. The child who does what is right, he shall live. The soul that sins shall suffer. Neither son nor father shall suffer for the iniquity of the other. The good man shall be rewarded and the wicked punished.

Some verses later comes the application of this principle:

> Israel complains: The Lord is not fair. My acting is not fair?! O, Israel. I will judge you . . . every one according to his ways of life. Return and repent . . . Cast away your sins. Change your heart for good and get a new spirit. I have no desire for anyone to die. Repent and live. (Ezekiel 18:19,20; 29–32)

To understand what is behind the ideas Ezekiel expresses here, we must consider what it means to be an exile or a refugee. The experience can make or break a person. There are those who lose heart completely and can only bewail their fate. Others resign themselves to getting along as best they can. For still others, misfortune becomes a challenge and an opportunity. Not content with simply adapting to the present, they reflect on the way they lived before, ponder on the ideas and plans they once took for granted, and begin to see everything about themselves in a new light.

That is what Ezekiel and those around him were doing. Certainly they must have spent many hours talking about the Scroll of the Law that had been found in the Temple during the time of King Josiah. They must have recalled the fervent celebration of the Feast of Passover and the extraordinary religious reformation that followed. And it well may be that thinking and talking about these memorable events led to the writing of Chapter 18 of the Book of Ezekiel. For it was the Babylonian exiles who began the regular meetings for reading and meditating on the Torah, and the work of gathering the prophetic writings that ultimately became part of what we know as the Bible. It was in this sacred heritage that the displaced Israelites found not only solace in misfortune but a new dedication to what was best in themselves.

The Synagogue: Beginnings in Babylonia

The exiles did not forget those of their neighbors and brothers who had stayed behind in the devastated land and cities of Judea. Without the Temple and a strong national leadership, what would become of them? Since they hoped one day to return, they also had other, more personal reasons for anxiety. For example, what if those who had stayed behind now claimed ownership of the land that had belonged to the exiles, and refused to give it up? Once again, it was Ezekiel who suggested the answer: *True, I have not banished them far away and scattered them in a foreign land, but I have been to them a little sanctuary in the countries where they have settled* (Ezekiel 11:15–16).

The prophet here assures the exiles that they are not to be deprived of what was theirs, and that God is with them even in a land far from their own. But this statement also contains what may be a clue to the origin of the synagogue. The Hebrew word *mikdash meaht,* translated as "little sanctuary," is believed by the rabbis to refer to the synagogue. It may be, as scholars have suggested, that the visits to the home of Ezekiel were a continuation of the visits the Israelites had made to the "man of God" on special days, as in the time of the prophets Samuel and Elisha. Be that as it may, tradition has it that the first synagogue ever built for the purpose of prayer was in Babylonia. According to Jewish legend, it was located in Nehardea, the first distinguished seat of learning, and was constructed near the House of Study of Ezra with the stones and the earth that had been transported from the Temple at Jerusalem—a sign of unbroken continuity.

Whatever truth there may be in the legend, there is no doubt that the city of Nehardea became one of the two greatest centers in Babylonia for the study of the Law. Undoubtedly it served as a place of worship and as a community center. There is also no doubt of the importance of leaders like Ezekiel in initiating the kind of thinking and talking and writing that evolved eventually into the Oral Law, or Talmud, side by side with the Written Law, the Torah. In Babylonia, too, the liturgy of the synagogue may well have begun to take form.

A Prophecy Fulfilled

Another inspiring forceful leader among the exiles was an extraordinary man whose name we do not know. He was a prophet of hope and solace. Comfortingly he assures his brothers that they will be delivered from Babylonia. Twice he even names the name of the redeemer: Cyrus the Great. In the synagogue today these chapters of consolation constitute the *Haftarah,* or prophetic selections, chanted at the end of the Torah reading, for a period of seven Sabbaths after the Fast of Tisha B'Av. He was the author of what is now the latter part of the Book of Isaiah. From what he wrote it is clear that he lived not less than a century and a half later than the Isaiah on whom King Hezekiah called for advice, and several decades later than Ezekiel. By that time, hope was strong among the exiles for the realization of their dream—the return to Jerusalem and the rebuilding of the Temple. This is the meaning behind the stirringly beautiful lines, at the beginning of Chapter 40:

Comfort ye, comfort ye my people, says your God. Speak ten-
derly to Jerusalem, and cry to her that her warfare is ended, that
her iniquity is pardoned.

Behind this joyful prophecy were events that had once again shaken the Middle East. Babylonia was dazed by the death of Nebuchadnezzar (605–562 B.C.E.), which set off a series of plots and assassinations that shook its very foundations. Its collapse was near. Now began the rise of Persia as a world power. (It in turn lasted for 200 years until the rise of Alexander the Great, 356–323 B.C.E., of Macedonia, Greece.) The new conqueror was Cyrus, founder of the Persian Empire. In the year 539 B.C.E. his armies entered the city of Babylon, and the rule of that empire came to an end. Of the great

Samaritan worship in Shechem (Nablus)

kings with whom the Jews came into contact, he was the first who was not an oppressor or a self-serving ally. Cyrus had sound ideas about how an empire should be governed; they were quite different from those of the warlike Assyrians and Babylonians. He believed that the countries constituting the new empire should have greater freedom in choosing their way of life. He respected the religions of the various peoples in his vast empire. Suiting action to belief, the generous liberator acted. In the year 538 B.C.E., a little more than fifty years after the Jews had been driven out of their homeland, Cyrus issued a decree that allowed the Jews to return, rebuild Jerusalem and restore the Temple. As a result, a total of 42,360 men, women and children above the age of twelve decided to leave Babylonia and make the journey back to Judea.

Once again, a miracle seemed to have taken place. The mood of joy and exultation in that far-off time has come down to us in a poem that we know as Psalm 126 (which is very familiar because on the Sabbath and festival days it is sung before the grace-after-meals):

> When the Lord brought the exiles back to Zion we were like men in a dream. Our mouths were filled with laughter and our voices shouted for joy. The nations said, "The Lord has done great things for His people. He has done great things with us. We are overjoyed . . ."

However, what they found when they returned to Jerusalem was not all joy and harmony. There were bitter antagonisms and secret plots, opposition and hatred by their enemies, and disunity among themselves. Once again, salvation might have ended in disaster but for the leadership of two great men, Ezra and Nehemiah, about whom we shall read in the next chapter. Thanks to them, the Temple was rebuilt and the Jewish nation revived under what is known as the Second Commonwealth. This was the period when Judaism was forged into the religion and the faith that have sustained the Jewish people through the two millennia that have since elapsed.

V

The Second Temple and the Synagogue

Return to Zion

The story of the return of the exiles who "went up to rebuild the House of God" is related in the books of Ezra and Nehemiah. It was not a mass exodus. We are told the names of the families who decided to make the journey while others chose to remain behind. The leaders of the first group to go were Sheshbazzar—whose name is Babylonian and who appears to have been a Prince of Captivity and by virtue of this office a member of the royal court at Babylon—as well as Zerubabel, a member of the Davidic dynasty, and the High Priest, Joshua. They took along, with the approval of the generous Cyrus, the gold and silver vessels that had been carried off by the soldiers of Nebuchadnezzar when the Temple was destroyed. But strange as it seems, there is no mention at all of the Ark. What had become of it? Had it been destroyed along with the Temple? All we know is that there was no Ark in the Second Temple which was erected in Jerusalem. As a matter of fact, it was no longer of prime significance to the returning exiles; the really important thing was their devotion to the Holy Scriptures and to the faith in the Covenant that had kept them together.

But the visible reality of the Temple they had dreamed of was important too. Of all the visions that came to Ezekiel, their first great leader, the most vivid had to do with the reconstruction of the Temple. Beginning with Chapter 40, the Book of Ezekiel gives a long and detailed description of the Temple as it would be rebuilt. The climax comes in a vision so intense that the prophet is overpowered:

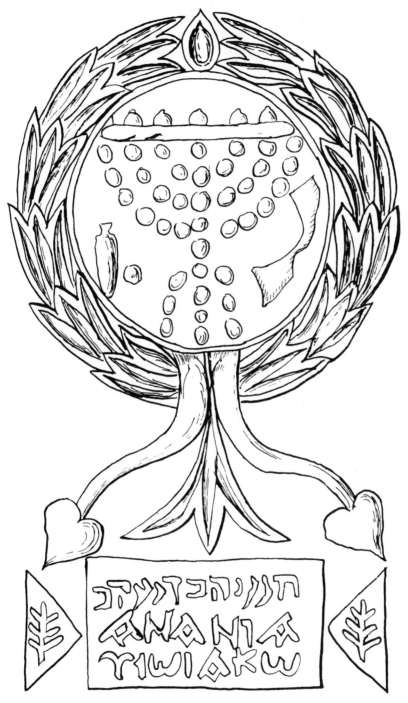

Seven-Branch Candelabrum carved in a grave in island of Malta. Note old Hebrew and Greek characters and ceremonial symbols

The glory of the God of Israel came from the east. His sound was like the sound of rushing waters and the earth shone with His splendor. And I fell upon my face. And behold the glory of the Lord filled the house. And He said, "Son of man, this is the place of My throne and the place of the soles of My feet, where I will dwell in the midst of the children of Israel forever. They shall never again defile My holy name by their abominations." (Ezekiel 43:2–9)

What the returning exiles actually found was very different from the splendor that Ezekiel had imagined. Like a river that is swallowed up by the desert sands, so the enthusiasm of the returnees spent itself. A beginning made in rebuilding the House of God was apparently the erection of the altar. But almost immediately trouble seems to have started with the descendants of those who had remained behind, and with the settlers from other lands who lived among them, the Samaritans. For many years they had lived with the Temple in ruins; and some of them felt no compulsion or eagerness to begin rebuilding it now. The returning exiles themselves were no doubt tempted to occupy themselves with the problems of settling down again in their previous home. Consequently, after the first spurt of enthusiasm, the work slowed down and as time passed it came to a full halt. It remained now, for a prophet to speak out. This time it was Haggai. In the book that is named for him we read:

In the second year of King Darius, God spoke to him [Haggai], to Zerubabel, Governor of Judea, and to Joshua the high priest, saying: "Thy people declare: 'The time has not yet come to rebuild the house of the Lord.' Is it a time for you yourselves to live in nice houses of your own while this house lies waste? . . . My house lies in ruins while each of you enjoys the pleasure of your own homes?" (Haggai 1:1–5, 9)

We know that Darius, who succeeded Cyrus as king of Persia, came to the throne in the year 521 B.C.E. Thus it was that in the year 520, eighteen years after the return of the first exiles from Babylon, the rebuilding got under way in earnest. This time the foundations were completed, and to mark the event a great celebration took place. The Book of Ezra records vividly the feelings, at once solemn and joyful, that marked this occasion:

When the builders laid the foundations, the priests in their apparel took their trumpets and the Levites their cymbals. Joyously they sang, alternating responses of praise and thanksgiving, "For he is good, for His mercy endures forever." All the people were exultant. (Ezra 3:10-11)

Again, however, there were difficulties, so that it was only in the "sixth year of Darius," or 515 B.C.E., that the rebuilding was finally completed, despite the malicious efforts of the governors of Syria and Samaria to block and prevent the work of building. As in the days of King Solomon, a feast of dedication followed. It was then that the priests and Levites throughout the country were assigned specific times when it would be their duty to take part in the sacrifice. This has a direct bearing on the founding of the synagogue, as will later be elucidated.

Nehemiah and Ezra: The Return of Two Exiled Leaders

Although worship in the Temple had been resumed, the city all around was still a sad place indeed. Physically, much of Jerusalem, including its gates and walls, was still in ruins. Socially, the returned exiles found themselves living side by side with Ammonities and Philistines, and this led to continual disturbances. A report of this unhappy situation reached one of the leading exiles who had remained in Babylonia. He was Nehemiah, a servant in the palace of Artaxerxes I, successor to Darius. As recounted in the Biblical book which bears his name:

In the month of Kislev, in the twentieth year, as I was in Shushan the castle, Hanani and a delegation from Jerusalem came to see me. I asked Hanani about the Jews and Jerusalem and they replied, "The remnant that are left of the captivity are in great trouble. The wall of Jerusalem is broken and the gates are burned and demolished." (1:1–3)

Indeed, the Jewish community of Jerusalem appeared to be disintegrating. The report so troubled Nehemiah that he asked the king for permission to journey to Jerusalem himself and there superintend the rebuilding of the city walls. The king having granted his permission, Nehemiah made the journey, and the work was begun. He met

with fierce opposition, especially from the Ammonites and from Sanballat, the governor of Samaria. The Samaritans had developed their
own version of the Jewish religion, with their own center of worship
on Mount Gerizim. (Here, even today, the few hundred Samaritans
now in Israel gather each year to celebrate the Passover.) As the Jews
would have nothing to do with the Samaritans or their religion,
Sanballat went so far as to try to persuade the Persian king that
Nehemiah was not to be trusted. Despite his opposition, however, in
the year 443 B.C.E. the work of rebuilding the city walls was at last
completed.

Meanwhile, a new leader had made his return from among the
exiles in Babylon—Ezra, "a scribe skilled in the law of Moses" (Ezra
7:6). Like Nehemiah, he came with the authority of the Persian ruler
to supervise the rebuilding of the city. The event that now took
place, on Rosh Hashanah in the year 444 B.C.E., marks another
milestone in Jewish history. The account that has come down to us
contains echoes of the dedication of the Temple during the reign of
King Solomon. What is more, it recalls the long-forgotten scroll that
was discovered in the Temple during the reign of King Josiah. We
read in Nehemiah, Chapter 8, the moving story of Ezra's reading the
Torah to the assembly and of his listeners' reaction, as well as Nehemiah's participation in this memorable event.

Ezra was now recognized as the spiritual leader of the Jewish
people. Thanks to him, the Torah, the Book of the Law, once again
became the great force that bound the children of Israel together.
The rabbis speak of Ezra as "the second founder of Judaism." In fact,
they say, "Ezra was worthy to have the Torah given to Israel through
him, had not Moses preceded him." It was thanks to Ezra and to the
Anshe Knesset Hagedolah (The Men of the Great Assembly) that the
Law of Moses was recorded in the form in which it has come down
to us. The Men of the Great Assembly were a body of religious
spiritual leaders who succeeded the prophets in the chain of the
Tradition. With Ezra they fixed the text of the Five Books of Moses
and transcribed it into the square Hebrew script which is in use
to-day. They also were the first to draw up the basic liturgy of our
present prayer book. Until then, knowledge of the Torah in ancient
Israel had been mainly limited to the Rabbis, Priests and Levites who
had charge of the Temple service. The celebration in 444 B.C.E.
marked a significant turning point. The Torah became the common

Restoration of Jerusalem and the Second Temple (located near the Holy Land Hotel, Jerusalem)

possession of the entire Jewish people. It is now read in the synagogue at least three days a week (on Saturday twice and on Monday and Thursday). The synagogue institution, as we shall see, made it all possible.

Worthy of note is the fact that this memorable assembly met in the broad place at the "water gate," not on the Temple Mount. Was it to signify that a gathering of worshipers could be held at any place?

The Ma-amadot

In the early days of the Second Temple, the daily sacrifice, known as the *Korban Tamid,* had been a private ceremony, paid for by a few wealthy men. Most of them belonged to the group known as the Sadducees, who were the aristocracy and landed gentry among the Jews. Like people of wealth and prestige in any age, they tended to be conservative, content to keep things as they were. Opposed in their thinking to the Sadducees were the Pharisees, who were mainly farmers and ordinary working people. They cared enough about the Temple to believe that the services there ought to represent all the Children of Israel, and not merely the rich and the aristocratic among them. This latter belief eventually prevailed, since the Pharisees dominated the thinking of the Judeans and constituted the majority.

The change was brought about by a new custom, based on a rotating assignment of the priests and Levites throughout the land. For this purpose the country had been divided into twenty-four regions, corresponding to the various categories and duties of the priesthood. We learn from I Chronicles 23:28–32 what some of these were. In addition to those directly concerned with the sacrifices and the Temple furnishings, they included guards, officials and a large number of musicians. Under the system of rotating assignments, the Priests and Levites of each region presumably spent one week each during the winter and summer in Jerusalem, performing the daily sacrifice at the Temple.

In the Book of Numbers (28:2) we find an ordinance implying that "all Israel" was to be present at the sacrifice. Since it was not possible for everyone to be present at the actual sacrifice, the Pharisees proposed that when the priests of a given section went to Jerusalem for their turn in presiding over the sacrifice at the Temple, a group of ordinary citizens should accompany them, to stand by during the week the priests were on duty. These groups of laymen were known in Hebrew as *Ma-amadot*, meaning "posts" or "select men." While they were in Jerusalem, those who had stayed home would gather in their towns and villages to read the parts of the Torah related to the sacrifice, and the verses from the story of creation in the Book of Genesis (Chapter 1) assigned to the particular day of the week. In addition, they apparently offered some prayers of their own. Thus began the custom of gathering regularly twice a day, morning and afternoon. Three such religious gatherings took place on the Sabbath, and four on the Day of Atonement, as they do in synagogues throughout the world even today. This explains why certain scholars, as for example Prof. Solomon Zeitlin of Dropsie University (Philadelphia, Pa.) look upon the *Ma-amadot* as the real origin of the synagogue.

From this it is clear that the synagogue was never regarded as a competitor to the Temple, but rather as a sort of extension of it. In fact, the Second Temple itself contained a room used as a synagogue. Known as the Hall of Hewn Stones, it was the place where the High Court met and where the *Ma-amadot* stood by and where the priests publicly recited the Shema while the sacrifice was taking place. It was used as well for public discussions and the reading of the Torah. It was built in the shape of a basilica and furnished the pattern for the early synagogues. The mere existence of such a room within the Temple was a sign of victory for the common people over those who believed in special privileges for the wealthy upper classes and the priests. It appears that its presence was an indication that the Temple was incomplete unless the people had a place for worship therein. There can be little doubt that the experience of the exiles who had gathered in little groups at the home of Ezekiel and in other places had made this triumph possible.

So it was that one by one, synagogues came to be built wherever Jews gathered for the study of the Torah. In the larger towns, from very early times, men belonging to the same trade or profession organized and built their own synagogues where they and their colleagues assembled for worship. (This practice has continued until very recent times.) In Jerusalem, synagogues were founded by groups of families who had been neighbors during the Babylonian exile. Moreover, every village, no matter how small, had at least one synagogue. All this was possible because, unlike the Temple, the synagogue was not a priestly institution. Any man who knew how to read the Torah was allowed to lead the service. What is more, only ten men—a *minyan**—were needed to form a synagogue. If a priest happened to be present, he would be especially honored perhaps by being called up first to read from the Torah. (As we noted in Chapter I, this ancient custom is still practiced today.)

But the service was conducted by ordinary people, and interpreted by the people who knew Hebrew, the language of the Torah. Because the synagogue was the place where the Torah was read, it became the real home of Jewish learning and religious education, from which the message of the Torah and the Prophets was spread. It was the place to which everyone went to pray, to study, and to consider matters of charity and law, of community and social welfare. Its appearance marked a new milestone in the history of the Jews.

The Exodus from Egypt had transformed a little group of tribes into a nation. The Babylonian exile had changed the nation into a religious community. Henceforward, as history ran its course, it would no longer be a people confined within the borders of Judea but would transcend statehood and its bonds. As that people became more and more widely scattered, new population centers sprang up outside the Land, eventually overshadowing it in number, and sometimes even in the quality of leadership and learning. They were living proof that the faith of Israel would live on, independent of a visible sanctuary.

Thus, an institution born in a strange land became rooted and flowered in the very shadow of the Temple in Jerusalem. When, in the year 70 C.E., the Second Temple was destroyed, the synagogue institution was on hand ready to carry on as its worthy successor.†

*Religious quorum. A religious gathering was called *edah*. In Numbers 14:27 the ten spies (exclusive of Joshua and Caleb) are named *edah*—hence this regulation. *Minyan* means number. For additional references on the significance of the number *ten* read Genesis 18:16–33; Numbers 14:26,27; 20:22; Leviticus 22:32,32.
†For an illuminating discussion on this entire period read Salo W. Baron's *The Jewish Community*, Vol. I, Chapter III.

VI

Destruction and Upheaval: The Synagogue Carries On

The Ptolemies

To understand the turbulent events that led to the final destruction of the Second Temple and its effect on the development of the synagogue, we must look once again at the rise and fall of empires and conquerors in the ancient world. The most sweeping conquests were made by Alexander the Great (356–323 B.C.E.). Upon his death, a contest began among his generals to determine who would control his empire.

For more than a century, Judea was ruled by the Ptolemies of Egypt. (It is estimated that there were about 1,000,000 Jews in Egypt). During this era, Greek came to be the language most commonly spoken throughout the ancient world. The impact of language led to the influences of Greek architecture and art, Greek ways of thinking and ways of life. All of this exercised a strong effect on the Jews, even though the Ptolemies, like Cyrus, made it their policy not to interfere in the religious observances and customs of their subjects.

In some ways, the Ptolemies seem actually to have encouraged the religion of the Jews. It was during their reign that a translation of the Hebrew scriptures into Greek, known as the Septuagint, was begun in Alexandria, the Egyptian city which was the greatest cultural center of the empire as well as the largest Jewish community. It was by means of this translation that the heritage of the Jews penetrated into the learning and civilization of Europe, greatly influencing Christianity and the Western world.

Temples Outside Jerusalem

There are indications that during the reign of the Ptolemies, many thousands of Jews left Palestine to settle in Egypt. Others had already been living there at least since the days of Persian rule. Thanks to the discovery of a number of letters written on papyrus and preserved through the centuries, we know that one such colony was in existence as early as the sixth century B.C.E. It was located in Yeb or Elephantine, near what is now Aswan. (Aswan is at the southern end of the country; there the huge dam is now located.) Surprisingly enough, this Jewish colony was a military garrison, manned by Jewish soldiers serving in the Persian army. Even more surprising is the evidence that at some time before 525 B.C.E. the Jews of this remote outpost had built a temple of their own which in many ways resembled the Temple of Jerusalem. Except for the exclusion of animal sacrifices the service seems to have been much the same as in Jerusalem.

According to a description that has survived, the temple at Elephantine, like its revered Jerusalem model, stood on a prominent site. It had five gateways and was roofed with cedar. Moreover, the ritual there was identical with that in Jerusalem. Jewish law, as we have noted, expressly forbade the offering of sacrifice anywhere except in Jerusalem. Yet these Egyptian Jews were evidently God-fearing men who would not intentionally have disobeyed the laws of the Torah. How, then, is the existence of the temple at Elephantine to be explained?

No one can be entirely sure. One explanation may be that at the time the colony was founded, the law set forth in the Book of Deuteronomy was not strictly observed. Another possibility is that the temple at Elephantine had already been built before the year 621 B.C.E., when during the reign of King Josiah the long-hidden scroll of the Torah was found. At any rate, in 410 B.C.E. the temple at Elephantine was destroyed by the Egyptian authorities in collaboration with the Persian officials who then ruled the country. Among ancient manuscripts from Elephantine is a letter addressed by the Jews of the military colony to Bagoas, the Persian governor of Judea, asking for his help in obtaining the permission of the authorities to have their temple rebuilt and the worship there restored. So far as we know, their request was not granted.

Similarly, it is known that more than two centuries later, around

170 B.C.E., yet another temple was built in Egypt. The ruins are in the town of Leontopolis. Modeled after the Temple in Jerusalem, it was built under the leadership of Onias II, a former high priest of Jerusalem who had fled following a dispute within the Jewish community.

These and other synagogue structures erected in the early Diaspora period were impressive in their appearance and ornamentation. Women too played an important role. "We find women bearing such titles as *Mother of the Synagogue,* and *President of the Synagogue.* In the centuries that followed, however, their prestige waned and diminished."*

Dissension and Rebellion

By then the easygoing tolerant rule of the Ptolemies had come to an end. Following the defeat of the Egyptian forces by the Seleucids, the Syrian Greeks, in 198 B.C.E., the Jews were ordered by force to accept Greek customs and the Greek ways of life.

There were some who favored compromise, even in religious matters. (It may have been a conflict over this question that led to the flight of Onias II, the "broadminded" high priest, and the building of the above-mentioned temple at Leontopolis.)

As the story is told in the First Book of Maccabees, *All the Gentiles accepted the command of the king. Many even from Israel gladly adopted his religion; they sacrificed to idols and profaned the Sabbath* (1:43). But many others refused to conform; and on the fifteenth of Kislev in the year 168 B.C.E. they heard with horror the news that the Temple had been desecrated by the pagan worship of Zeus, the chief god of the Greeks. What followed was the first organized persecution of the Jews, a grim portent of things to come:

> The books of the law which they found they tore to pieces and burned with fire. Where the Book of the Covenant was found in the possession of any one, or if any one adhered to the law, the decree of the King condemned him to death . . . But many in Israel stood firm and were resolved in their hearts not to eat unclean food. They chose to die rather than to be defiled by food or profane the holy covenant; and they did die . . . (I Maccabees)

*Essay by Saul Lieberman, *The Jewish Expression*, New York, Bantam Books, 1970.

In this time of crisis a priestly family, the Hasmoneans, also called Maccabeans, took the lead in a revolt against the Syrian oppressors. The pious sect known as *Hasidim*, together with all believing Jews, rallied behind these patriots, who—in the words of a noted Biblical scholar, W.F. Albright—"struggled with an energy and a zeal seldom approached and perhaps never surpassed in history," As a result of the struggle, in the year 165 B.C.E. the Temple was purified once more—an event annnually celebrated ever since as Hanukkah, the Feast of Lights.

The struggle, however, was not ended; it was to continue for many years longer before the Jews were able to worship without interference. Under Simon, a Hasmonean who was high priest from 143 to 135 B.C.E., the independence they had fought for at last became a reality. Then, beginning with Aristobulus, who ruled in 104 and 103 B.C.E., the Hasmoneans became kings as well as priests. This aggrandizement of power was unwelcome to many Jews. It became an important factor in the disagreement between the Pharisees, who opposed the monarchy, and the Sadducees, who favored it.

The Last Days of the Temple

The independent Jewish state ruled by the Hasmoneans lasted until 40 B.C.E., and as the decades passed, these rulers became progressively more cruel and oppressive. One of their final achievements was to conquer the Edomites, a pagan people who inhabited the territory east and south of the Jordan, and to force them to be circumcised and to worship as Jews. In the meantime, Rome had become the ruling power in the Mediterranean world. In the year 63 B.C.E. the armies of the Roman general Pompey entered Jerusalem and laid siege to the Temple. They slaughtered the priests, but out of reverence they did not enter the sanctuary.

After the Hasmonean dynasty collapsed, Herod the Great—a prince of Edom, whose people had been forced to convert to Judaism —was crafty enough to gain the favor of the Roman Emperor. As a result, in the year 37 B.C.E. he was crowned king of the Jews. His reign was one of inhuman cruelty and elaborate building projects, the most ambitious of which was the rebuilding of the Temple in Jerusalem. Although it was not religious motives that moved him, he took care not to offend the sentiments of devout Jews. Begun in the eighteenth year of his reign, the rebuilding was completed ten years later, in 9 B.C.E. Constructed of white stone, the Temple was adorned with gold, and covered with a roof of cedarwood. The approaches to it were by a number of gates and bridges and it was surrounded by a large wall, remnants of which are extant to this day. The Western Wall, in old Jerusalem, the most hallowed spot of the Jewish people, is a remnant of this wall. The project employed 10,000 workers, including a thousand priests specially trained as stonemasons. The women's section was built on the ground floor; it had three entrances reserved exclusively for women. The new Temple area was twice as large as the old had been. Standing within what was known as the Court of the Gentiles, it was set on a raised terrace surrounded by a high stone balustrade, on which were warning inscriptions in Greek and Latin, such as: *Strangers are forbidden to pass the barrier and enter the precincts of the sanctuary. Anyone found doing so will himself be responsible for the death penalty which will be inflicted on him.* Around the Temple Gate were terraces where the prophets expounded (Jeremiah 7:2).

During the reign of Herod and the Roman procurators who followed him, riots and disorders increased as the anger of the Jewish people grew more intense against the invaders. Rebel leaders went into hiding or were hunted down, only to have others rise in their place. In the summer of 66 C.E., the smoldering revolt at last burst into flames. The war lasted seven bloody years. The last stronghold to fall was Masada, where a small garrison held out until the year 73.

Three years prior to that surrender, the Emperor Titus had entered Jerusalem and destroyed everything, including the Temple. Just over half a century later, during the reign of Hadrian, there was one last desperate uprising. It was led by Simon Bar Kochba, who succeeded in taking Jerusalem from the Romans but lost it again in 135. Renamed as the Roman colony Aelia Capitolina, the conquerors replaced the Temple with a shrine honoring Zeus and the Emperor, whom the Romans worshiped as a god. The sacred place it had usurped has since then never been rebuilt.

The Dome of the Rock

Where the Temple once stood, modern-day visitors will find a Moslem shrine, known as the Dome of the Rock or Mosque of Omar, so named after the Caliph Omar, who is said to have built a sanctuary there in 638. When the Crusaders took Jerusalem in the eleventh century, they converted it into a church, calling it *Templum Domini*, the Temple of the Lord. (It was from this shrine that the Knights Templar took their name.) In 1187, when the Crusaders were driven out by the Egyptian Sultan Saladin, it once again became a mosque.

Inside, enclosed by a gleaming mosaic-covered dome, is the *Sakhra*, or Rock, from which Moslems believe Mohammed ascended to heaven. Jewish tradition associates it with the altar built by David on the threshing floor of Araunah the Jebusite (II Samuel, 24). And scholars think the sacred bronze altar of the Temple may have been located on the Rock. There is a small cave underneath, which Moslems believe to be inhabited by spirits. According to a Jewish legend, it was here that the sacred vessels of the Temple were hidden at the time of its destruction.

Ancient Remains in Palestine

And what of the synagogue? Until recently, evidence of its presence in those early years came to us from literary records. Thus, from the Mishnah (Yoma 7) we learn of the one that was built on the Temple grounds. Although no traces have yet been found of the building itself, as stated above excavations in the area have uncovered an inscription in Greek stating that Theodotos ben Vettenos, son and grandson of its presiding elder, had built it, as well as an inn with rooms and a water supply for travelers who had come from a distance to worship at the Temple. The Jerusalem Talmud speaks in one place of a total of 394 synagogues in the city of Jerusalem itself; in another, the number cited is no less than 480.

Until about a hundred years ago, references in post-Biblical literature such as the Talmud (as well as the New Testament) were the only source of information concerning the synagogue in Palestine. It was known, for example, that wherever possible the synagogue was located on the highest spot in town. According to the rabbis, a city whose roofs overtopped the synagogue was destined to be destroyed. Later, in Babylonia and throughout the Diaspora this practice had to be abandoned to maintain peaceful relations with the non-Jewish neighbors. We know also that synagogues were generally located near running water, to allow worshipers to wash their hands and

Capernaum—remains of the synagogue

cleanse themselves before entering. With the advent of Christianity, which regarded Jesus as the Messiah, a parting of the ways began. Little by little the Jewish Christians were alienated from the congregation of Israel. Their exclusion was necessary to preserve the unity of the Jews and to prevent the Jewish faith from being swallowed up by Christianity.

Synagogue at Masada

Supplementing the literary record of the period are the impressive archeological discoveries constantly being made in Israel. The most dramatic find was made on the historic Rock of Masada by Prof. Yigael Yadin of the Hebrew University, a leading Israeli archeologist, in the middle 1960's. As stated above, Masada was the last outpost to fall in the Judean rebellion against Rome (73 C.E.). The story of the fall of Masada and of its heroic defenders, the Zealots, has thrilled and inspired Jews for nearly two thousand years and has enshrined Masada in the hearts of the Jewish people forever. Today Masada is one of the most popular attractions in modern Israel to Israelis and foreign tourists alike.

In 1966 Professor Yadin reported on his explorations.* One of his momentous Masada discoveries was a synagogue. Evidently it was erected later than the other buildings on a location where an earlier building had stood. It is the conjecture of Professor Yadin and his associates that the original building too had probably been a synagogue built by King Herod, who fortified Masada between the years 36–30 B.C.E. Its orientation to Jerusalem, its architectural plan, the findings there of remnants of very ancient scrolls comprised for Professor Yadin evidence that it had indeed been a synagogue. In the main, the general plan of the structure followed the architecture of the Galilean synagogues described below.

Only as late as February 15, 1972, the *Jerusalem Post* reported digging up a synagogue built in the third century C.E. at Ein Gedi, also near the Dead Sea. Found for the first time was a *kiyor*, or wash basin, of plastered stone for washing worshipers' hands and feet; it was located in the entrance hall.

Masada, New York, Random House, 1966. For the story of the synagogue in Herodium, near Jerusalem, read Yadin's *Bar Kokhba*, 1971, 184 ff.

Also discovered was a mosaic floor consisting of a geometric design around four peacocks and a border of peacocks and a seven-branched menorah. Measuring about 50 x 39 feet, the Ark was located in the northern wall facing Jerusalem. Another unique finding was an inscription in Aramaic, "Remember to the good all the people of this city"—the first and only one of its kind. The synagogue was destroyed sometime in the seventh century.

Galilean and Other Synagogues

The founding of the Palestine Exploration Society in 1870 made it possible to understand how the earliest synagogues looked. At the outset, as archeologists and scholars began their exploration of the Holy Land, they discovered a number of ruins which, judging by the ornate carved images and decorations that had survived, appeared to be pagan in origin. But the Hebrew and Aramaic inscriptions carved into the stone of these buildings made it unmistakably clear that these had in fact been Jewish houses of worship. Thus far, the remains of over fifty such buildings—dating from the second to the early part of the fourth century—have been uncovered. They are indeed a revelation, especially as regards the extent to which Greek and Roman art has influenced that of the Jews.

Earlier synagogues, built before 70 C.E., were destroyed by Titus during the Jewish War; and those built before 135 by Hadrian during the rebellion of Bar Kochba. Best preserved of those that remain are the ones in northern Galilee, not far from the borders of Syria and Lebanon. This location is no accident. By the end of the second century, as the survivors of the Bar Kochba revolt moved northward, Galilee had become the center of Jewish life in Palestine. At this time, the attitude of the Roman emperors toward the Jews was friendly, with the result—as the size and richness of the synagogue buildings suggest—that it was a prosperous period. The synagogues of this period were built on high ground. They usually consisted of a two-story building surrounded by a courtyard, with an outer staircase leading to an upper gallery for the women. It was built on three sides which were supported by columns. Usually the entrance doors in the front wall faced south toward Jerusalem.

The main prayer or assembly hall was built in the form of a basilica, a rectangular space divided by colonnades into a wide central nave and two side aisles. It was entered through a large central door, with two smaller doors opening onto the aisles. At the opposite end was a raised *bimah*, or platform, where the chest or ark containing the Torah scrolls was placed. This end faced toward Jerusalem, in accordance with the tradition that all worship should be directed toward the Temple. The floor was covered with flagstones.

One of the best preserved of these Galilean synagogues is the one known as *Kfar Biram* or *Bar'am*, seven miles northwest of Safed near the Lebanese border. Its three carved entrances, which are still intact, are richly decorated with bas-reliefs of vine leaves and grape clusters, palm branches, and the figures of animals. Indeed, the elaborate facade was the major feature of most Galilean synagogues.

Still more imposing is the synagogue at Kfar Nahum on the northern shore of Lake Kinneret, the Sea of Galilee—a name familiar to Christians, since it is associated with the early career of Jesus. The first chapter of the Gospel of Mark relates that Jesus and his disciples went into Capernaum, "and straightway on the Sabbath day he entered into the synagogue, and taught." It seems likely that the building where he preached was not far from the one uncovered by archeologists, dating to the second or third century, and reconstructed on the ruins of another built some centuries earlier. Rising above the blue waters of the lake, the two-story structure of white limestone masonry must have been an impressive sight. The remains are now cared for by members of the Franciscan order, who are hospitable to the many tourists and Israelis who visit it.

A few miles away are the remains of yet another synagogue, built of basalt masonry, in the ancient town of Chorazin. Little of it is left except for the so-called Seat of Moses, the chair occupied during the service by an elder singled out for that honor, and fragments of two carved stone lions that evidently stood on either side of the Torah shrine.

The peaceful period in Galilee did not last long. When the power of Rome was replaced in the Near East by the Byzantine Empire, around the beginning of the fourth century, the atmosphere in Palestine changed from one of tolerance to one of suspicion and animosity. This change appears to be reflected in the synagogues themselves. Outwardly they were no longer ornate or imposing—as though to avoid notice—but inside, where they had once been plain, they were richly ornamented.

This change is seen most vividly in an ancient synagogue excavated at Bet Shearim in the western part of the Valley of Jezreel. The structure combines a building dating to the first half of the third century with alterations and reconstruction made in the fourth. The most striking alteration involved blocking up the central door of the original building and replacing it with an apse, a vaulted semi-circular recess for the Ark of the Torah that was fixed in the wall. In earlier buildings, the box containing the scroll had been movable. Indeed, the Talmud mentions that in some places the Torah scrolls were placed in private homes for safekeeping. There was also another

Remains of Chorazin Synagogue, Galilee

more significant change: the rear wall (not the front wall) faced Jerusalem. The congregants now entered at the opposite end of the nave and sat facing the Ark—looking, that is, toward Jerusalem. We know that in the earliest synagogues the Ark containing the Torah scrolls was not kept in the main hall but in the adjoining room or alcove, from which it was brought out for the public reading of the Torah.* The practice of placing the Torah Ark on the wall facing toward Jerusalem, which seems to have begun around the fourth century, has continued to the present day.

Another change that took place at this time was in the form of the decorations. In the earliest synagogue remains that have thus far been found, they consisted of sculpture and stone carvings. In the remains at Bet Shearim, we see the transition from stone to mosaic and frescoed walls. Because Bet Shearim originally served as the seat of the Sanhedrin, i.e., the Supreme Court and Legislature and one of the great centers of Torah learning, it could very well have exerted a strong influence on other synagogue buildings both in Palestine and beyond.

Much the same interior arrangement and decoration were found in Palestine synagogues which had been built more than two centuries later. A splendid example is the Bet Alpha synagogue, discovered in the Jezreel valley by a kibbutz crew who were at work on an irrigation ditch late in the winter of 1928.

When the excavation of Bet Alpha was completed, it was found that the most spectacular thing discovered there was a mosaic floor. In colors that were still bright after so many centuries, it depicted Helios, the sun-god, riding a chariot of a kind frequently shown in Greek art, in a design encircled by the symbols of the Zodiac. Nearby is a smaller mosaic showing the sacrifice of Isaac. An inscription dates the work to the reign of the Roman emperor Justin (518–527). Built of rough limestone blocks in varying sizes, the building was much smaller than the Bar'am synagogue. But what made the discovery so intriguing was the subject matter of the decoration. The prohibition of the Second Commandment—"Thou shalt not make any graven image for yourselves" (Exodus 20:4)—seems not to have applied to carved figures showing plants and animals.

---

*Some scholars are of the opinion that this explains the custom of the procession of the Torah when it is taken out and returned to the Ark.

Beth Shearim, entrance to the Catacombs

Bar'am remains of façade and portico

Bet Alpha—mosaic of the synagogue floor

Until the twentieth century there was no known instance of the use of human figures in the art works within a Jewish house of worship except for Dura-Europos described below. This prohibition was in accordance with the Second Commandment. The Jewish historian, Flavius Josephus, tells in his *Antiquities* (Book XVII) how a group of young men sacrificed their lives in order to pull down an eagle that had been placed by Herod above the entrance to the Temple in Jerusalem. He explains that they did so not only because of its idolatrous nature but chiefly because it was a symbol of Roman rule. It would appear, however, that as the Jews came into more intimate contact with the civilizations of Greece and Rome, their concern with the strict prohibition of images diminished because these had ceased to symbolize Roman rule. Thus we find a statement in the Jerusalem Talmud that at the time of Rabbi Jochanan—that is, in the third century C.E.—Jews began to have paintings on the wall, and the rabbis did not hinder them from doing so, presumably because these were now divested of their original significance, and were intended mainly for decoration, not for worship. Evidently the Greek-Roman idolatry practices no longer presented any threat.

Dura-Europos Murals

That Jews had also begun to have paintings on the walls of their synagogues emerged from the findings of one of the major archeological explorations of this century, the excavation of the ruins of Dura-

Dura Europos: Panel Depicting Ezekiel's Prophecy of the Dead Bones (Ch. 37)

אריה

בתולה

שבתי

דגים

Hamat—Tiberias, floor mosaic in zodiac design
Sardis, Turkey—remains of an ancient synagogue

Europos in eastern Syria. Never an important center in itself, this ancient town situated on the right bank of the Euphrates River lay on the trade route between Baghdad to the east and Aleppo to the west. It had been built as a fortress under the Seleucids and had been conquered by the Romans in 165 C.E.. When, not quite a century later, the Sassanid rulers of Persia laid siege to the fort, the Romans heaped sand and clay between its walls and the houses within them for protection. One result of this was that this accumulation of dirt preserved an entire city block almost intact. Among the buildings discovered by the expedition was one that had clearly been a synagogue. A single room (14 x 8 yards) with a capacity for about ninety persons, men and women, it was larger than the Christian church that stood near-by, and so well preserved that the holes in the floor that had once held the legs of lampstands were still plainly to be seen. The most remarkable finds in synagogue archeology were the murals that covered its walls. Arranged in horizontal rows above a frieze of animals, masks, and geometric designs, they depicted the patriarchs, prophets, kings, queens, and heroes of the Bible.

An inscription found on the building dates it at around 244–245 C.E. It served but some 12 years. Coins discovered during the excavation indicate that an earlier synagogue had existed here, built probably between 165 and 200 C.E. A modest building, the earlier synagogue seems to have served as a dwelling and as an inn for Jewish wayfarers. Unlike the Galilean synagogues of the same period, it did not contain an upper women's gallery; instead, the women may have been seated in a separate room alongside the main hall. No trace was found of a partition between the men's and women's sections. A niche built in the middle of its western wall shows where the Ark was placed when the Torah was brought in. The synagogue faced the west in the direction of Jerusalem.

Although the buttressing of the walls inadvertently saved the Dura synagogue and its murals for posterity, it did not save the Romans from the onslaught of the Sassanid (Persian) invaders. The city was destroyed, in the third century, and the survivors of the battle were routed or taken prisoner. What became of the Jewish community that had worshiped there is unknown. There is some evidence to suggest that they had time to gather up the Ark, the scrolls, and the lampstands as they fled. Which way they went— eastward toward Babylon, westward toward Judea—no one can say. The only trace of them is in the synagogue they left behind.

Synagogue Of Sardis

A truly outstanding synagogue of the second or third century was excavated at Sardis—a major Roman city situated some 60 miles inland from Izmir, West Turkey. Izmir is also known as Smyrna; it is a large seaport on the Aegean Sea. Some scholars maintain Sardis had already been in existence during the period of the Persian Empire; certain it is that it dates to the second century C.E., as will be shown later.

The synagogue was discovered in the summer of 1962 during the excavations carried on by the universities of Harvard and Cornell. Compared with the one at Ostia* this synagogue was immense and magnificent. The main hall of the assembly measured 300 by 60 feet, reminding one of the Alexandrian edifice. All the other architectural features were commensurate—the roof, the ornate mosaic floor, the paneled marble walls and so on. At the western end of the hall was a spacious apse, containing curving rows of three brick benches; they were very likely the seats of the elders. The walls of the hall were decorated with illustrated inlays of fish, birds, animals and flowers. It is conjectured that there had also been paintings on them as in those of Dura Europos. A marble basin was located in the forecourt for the washing of the hands and perhaps the feet as well. To the east stood a large marble table. It was supported by columns decorated with eagles. Also to the east were elevated platforms—possibly one for the *Aron Kodesh,* the other for the menorah. The latter contained carvings of the *lulav* and *etrog* (palm branch and citrus).

An extraordinary feature of the synagogue is that it preserved fragments of relics and inscriptions which had apparently been found in the pagan temples and sanctuaries of Sardis dating back hundreds of years, possibly as early as the sixth century B.C.E. These were incorporated in the structure and ornamentation. From the antiquities found next to the synagogue, such as pottery jars with the inscriptions of names on them, it is surmised that this religious center was also the marketplace and commercial center.

The many inscriptions, in Greek, of the names of the donors found all over the place date the synagogue to the late second and early third centuries. Many names end with the honorable title *Sar-*

*See Chapter VII.

dianos meaning Citizen of Sardis; several carry the information that the owners were members of the city council. Also very striking and exceptional is the very site of the synagogue. It seems to have been an integral part of the Roman city complex containing the sports arena, the recreation halls and city center of Sardos. Indeed at first the building had been mistaken as a large public center, but the discoveries of Hebrew inscriptions identified it as a Jewish house of worship.

The conclusions of the findings thus far—the excavation and reconstruction are continuing—is the irrefutable evidence of the existence of a large prosperous and respected Jewish community in the Eastern Roman Empire. It was allowed to build a house of worship on the main avenue in the most important spot of the city. And it rose to the challenge by erecting a magnificent edifice worthy of Sardis Jewry to both the tradition and the host city. It is proof and testimony to the tolerance exercised by the Roman government to its subjects in the early centuries of the Christian era.

VII

The Ancient Synagogue, School and Community Center

Jewish Self-Government

There are three names for synagogue in Hebrew: *Bet Tefilah,* a House of Prayer; *Bet Hamidrash,* a House of Study; and *Bet Haknes-set,* a House of Assembly. The word "synagogue" is from the Greek and means assembly. In the Babylonian Talmud the synagogue is referred to most often as *Bet Haknesset.* (The Hebrew word used today for the Parliament of Israel is Knesset.) From the popular usage of this name it is evident that the synagogue has always been the center of Jewish life communally, religiously and educationally.

In the regions under the control of the Persian rulers, and later of the Moslems, the scattered communities of Jews living in the east of Palestine were largely free to govern themselves, and the center of self-government was the synagogue. This arrangement continued for about a thousand years, from the second until the twelfth century. During this long period the chief Jewish official was the Exilarch, a descendant of the House of David, who represented his people and served as an adviser to the Persian "King of Kings" and to their successors, the Moslem caliphs. From his seat at Bagdad his authority extended throughout Arabia and eastward as far as the borders of India. His chief counselors were the *Geonim,* the heads of the great Talmudical Academies, founded at Sura in 219 and at Pumpeditha around 259. The Academies were, in fact, not only centers of learning but also legislative bodies and courts of law.

The Gaon of Sura took the Exilarch's place when he was absent, and at his death served as regent until a successor could be chosen.

This was done at a gathering in Bagdad of the heads of the Academies, their disciples, and the elders of the Jewish community. The installation of a newly appointed Exilarch took place in the synagogue. A vivid description of the ceremony has come down to us from a tenth-century writer, Nathan HaBavli who describes the event thus:

> On Thursday they [members of the Jewish Community] assembled in the synagogue, blessed the Exilarch, and placed their hands on him. They blew the shofar, that all the people, small and great, might hear. When the people heard the proclamation, every member of the community sent him a present, according

Ancient Color Glass from the Talmudic period (note Torah rolls lying horizontally in Ark)

to his power and means. All the heads of the community and the wealthy members sent him magnificent clothes and beautiful ornaments, vessels of silver and vessels of gold, each man according to his ability. The Exilarch prepared a banquet on Thursday and on Friday, serving all kinds of food. . . .

When he arose on Sabbath morning to go to the synagogue, many of the prominent men of the community met him and accompanied him. At the synagogue a wooden pulpit had been prepared for him on the previous day, the length of which was seven cubits, and the breadth of which was three cubits.* They spread over it magnificent coverings of silk, blue, purple and scarlet, so that it was entirely covered, and nothing was seen of it. Now there entered under the pulpit distinguished young men, well versed in the prayers and all that appertains to them. The Exilarch was concealed in a certain place together with the heads of the Academies and the youths stood under the pulpit. No man sat there. The precentor [prayer leader] of the synagogue would begin the prayer *Barukh Sheamar*—"Blessed be he who spoke "—and the youths, after every sentence of that prayer, would respond: *Barukh Hu*—"Blessed be He." When he chanted the Psalm of the Sabbath Day [Psalm 92], they responded after him: *It is good to give thanks unto the Lord.* All the people together read the "verses of song,"** until they finished them. The precentor then arose and began the prayer *Nishmat Kol Hai*—† "The breath of all living," and the youths responded after him: "shall bless Thy name"; he chanted a phrase, and they responded after him, until they reached the *Kedushah*, which was said by the congregation in a low voice, and by the youths in a loud voice . . . When all the people were seated, the Exilarch came out of the place where he was concealed. Seeing him come out, all the people stood up, until he sat down on the pulpit, which had been made for him. The head of the Academy of Sura came out after him, and after exchanging courtesies with the Exilarch, sat down on the pulpit. Then the head of the Academy of Pumbeditha came out, and he, too, bowed, and sat down at his left.

*A cubit is about one and one-half feet.
**Introductory part of morning prayers.
†The so-called doxology that introduces the Sabbath prayers.

During all this time the people stood upon their feet, until these three were properly seated. At his place, over his head, above the pulpit, they spread a magnificent covering, fastened with cords of fine linen and purple. Then the precentor put his head under the Exilarch's canopy in front of the pulpit, and with blessings that had been prepared for him on the preceding days he blessed him in a low voice, so that he should be heard only by those who sat around the pulpit, and by the youths who were under it. When he blessed him, the youths responded after him in a loud voice: "Amen!" All the people were silent until he had finished his blessings. . . .*

From the above description we can readily see that a synagogue liturgy was already in existence. Some years after the destruction of the Temple in 70 C.E., Rabbi Gamaliel II partially fixed the "canon" of the Liturgy and the periods of daily prayer: morning, afternoon and evening. Prayer, of course, helped unite the people, preserved the Hebrew language and kept alive the memory of the Land of Israel. It ensured the oneness of the people. Early prayer was oral and was recited by heart. In Babylonia the heads of the Academies brought about the first written order of prayers, or Siddur. (The word *siddur* means order.) Indeed, Rab Amram Gaon of Babylonia is the father of the Prayer Book that is in use today. In setting down the exact arrangement and content of the prayers recited in Babylonia on the weekdays, on Sabbaths and Festivals, and on fastdays, and even the Haggadah Service at the Passover Seder, he bequeathed the Prayer Book to future generations.

Synagogue as School

Just as in Babylonia where the synagogue probably grew out of those long-ago meetings of the exiles at the house of Ezekiel, so the great future Academies of Sura and Pumbeditha evolved simultaneously into houses of study. It was thanks to the study and preservation of the sacred Scriptures that the great collection of scholarly commentaries which comprise the Babylonian Talmud came into being. Similar academies were connected with the Sanhedrin, the highest court and legislature, which were convened at various times in Jerusalem,

*B. Halper, *Post-Biblical Hebrew Literature,* Jewish Publication Society, Philadelphia.

Yavneh, Bet Shearim, Tiberias and other centers in Palestine. Their collection of commentaries is known as the Jerusalem Talmud.

The Jewish people's dedication to learning has been proverbial, and their commitment to the sacred writings, "the source of doctrine and conduct," led Mohammed (570–632 C.E.) to call them the People of the Book. For some, indeed, study ranked even above worship. One of them was Rab Hisda of the Sura Academy, who declared that prayer was a temporal act, concerned with the self and the present, whereas study dealt with what was eternal. Another Babylonian scholar, Rabbi Hammuna, holding the same view, reprimanded those who took a long time with their prayers; such persons, he said, neglect matters of eternity to busy themselves with things of the moment.

But knowledge of the Torah was never confined to the academies. In synagogues everywhere, the weekly reading of the Torah, which from early times was often followed by a sermon, was a means of instructing the entire community. Along with this instruction, dating also from very early times, went the education of children. According to a tradition recorded in the Talmud the city of Betar, Bar Kochba's last stronghold, allegedly had no less than four hundred synagogues, each with four hundred pupils; and when the invading Romans appeared, the students defended their lives with the wooden pointers which they used to guide their reading from the Torah scrolls. While this was probably an exaggeration, it reveals the state of mind and imagination of the people.

A leading historian of the Jewish school, the late Dr. Nathan Morris, writes that the synagogue remained inseparable from the Jewish school from the second to the tenth century. It was in such a school that the great Rabbi Akiba, at the age of forty, began to study Hebrew side by side with his own son. We are told that on a teaching-board—probably a tablet covered with wax on which letters were incised with a pointed stylus: *the teacher wrote out "aleph-bet" and they learned it, and so on to "aleph-tav" (the final letter), and they learned that . . . [then followed] the priestly book "Vayikra" [the first eight chapters of Leviticus] and they mastered it. And so they continued until they learned the whole Torah.*

In the tenth century, children are said to have studied from Torah scrolls that had been withdrawn from use because they were declared unfit for public reading. There is no doubt that study materials were rare and expensive. Whether the scrolls used in teaching were bought by the parents or remained the property of the school we do not know. We do know that each student set his own pace, reporting individually by reciting to the teacher and then returning to his place to continue his study on his own. The school was open every day except on the Sabbath, with a shorter session on Fridays in winter, when the ushering in of the Sabbath began at an early hour. This intensive schedule is followed to this day in the Orthodox Hebrew day schools and Yeshivot, or Talmudical academies.

Religious School and Community Center

The training of children in Torah and religious observance started even before they could walk. The mother of one famous rabbi, Joshua ben Hanania, is said to have brought his cradle to the synagogue school so that he could absorb Torah from his earliest years. *As soon as the youngster can wave,* the rabbis taught, *he is enjoined to wave the "lulav," [palm branch]; to wrap himself, he is to put on the "tallit" [prayer shawl]; to guard the "tephillin" [phylacteries], his father provides him with "tephillin."* Similarly, from the time they could speak, children were taught to recite the *Shema: Hear, O Israel: The Lord is our God, the Lord is one. And you shall love the Lord your God with all your heart, with all your soul, and with all your might,* and so on, as stated in Deuteronomy, Chapter 6.

Indeed, it was the unique role played by the synagogue in the Middle Ages that invested it with the name *schul.* The Yiddish term *schul* is derived from the German *Schule,* meaning school. This name is synonymous with synagogue to this day. We go to *schul* to *daven,* or worship, to hear a sermon, a discourse on the Torah. And in most communities we go to synagogue to attend a religious school and to participate in all its activities involving classroom study, club and recreational activities. The synagogue was also the courthouse to dispense justice. It was the place where prominent scholars and leaders were eulogized before burial. Sometimes it was a kind of "underground." Thus the historian Josephus records that the rebels met in the Great Synagogue in Tiberias to plan the uprising against Rome.

Center of Tzedakah

Hand in hand with the central role of teaching went another activity which is summed up in the single Hebrew word *tzedakah*, or charity —the obligation to give help to whoever may be in need. This is a Biblical tradition that dates back to Abraham, who offered food and rest to the three strangers as they approached his tent on the plains of Mamre. In the Talmud the rabbis devoted a good deal of thought to the concept of *tzedakah*, which they expanded and codified as relevant laws. They also created a new concept known as *Gemilut Hasadim*, loving-kindness, i.e., giving of one's self. We are told that after the destruction of the Temple of Jerusalem, two rabbis stood among the ruins. One, Rabbi Joshua, burst forth with a grief-stricken cry: *Woe to us, for the place where Israel prayed and atoned for its sins is destroyed!* Then the other, Rabbi Johanan ben Zakkai, who had escaped from Jerusalem and founded a center of learning in Yavneh, gave this answer: *Grieve not, my son, for we may atone by doing good deeds of loving kindness. For the Scripture says: desire mercy and not sacrifice!*

Throughout the centuries it was such concern for the welfare of all Jews that helped keep the Jewish people vigorously alive. From time immemorial to the present on Sabbath mornings Jews invoke the blessing of the Lord on all who, among the observance of other mitzvot, provide food for wayfarers and charity for the poor. Indeed, the Roman emperor Justinian (483–565 C.E.) took notice of this characteristic in his wondering comment that there were no beggars among the Jews of his time.

Concern for providing hospitality to wayfarers was expressed, as indicated above, in an inscription, the only remnant recording the existence of an ancient synagogue on the Temple grounds at Jerusalem: *Theodotos . . . , built the synagogue for the reading of the Law and for the teaching of the Commandments, and the chambers and the water installation for the lodging of needy strangers.*

Synagogue at Ostia

Provisions of this sort were also found in the excavation of an ancient synagogue at Ostia, now a summer resort at the mouth of the Tiber near Rome. It is today the seaside resort of Rome; in the days of the

Caesars it was a strong Jewish community. The town had originally been built by the Romans as a defense against invasion from the sea. In time it had become a thriving commercial port, whose people came from many places. That its inhabitants included a colony of Jews was not known until 1961, when the bulldozer of a highway construction crew unearthed the remains that turned out to be those of a synagogue.

Situated on what had been the waterfront of the ancient city, the building consisted of several sections, the earliest dating to around the end of the first century. Over the years a series of additions had been built, with a partial reconstruction in the fourth century. The synagogue's main entrance, facing a road that ran parallel to the shore, led into a narrow vestibule. On one side of this passageway

Ostia: Bas-relief of Menorah, Palm Branch (Lular) Etrog (citrus) and Ranis Horn (Shofar)

were a series of small rooms, which seem to have been used as lodgings for guests and possibly as schoolrooms. On the other side were two larger rooms. One contained an oven, which is presumed to have been used in baking unleavened bread for Passover, together with a marble-topped table—probably for kneading dough—and a row of large earthenware vats, in which wine, oil and other provisions are believed to have been kept.

The second and more spacious of the two larger rooms was the prayer hall, measuring about forty by eight feet. Its ceiling was supported by columns of gray marble, with white marble bases and capitals, and its floor was paved with black and white mosaic inlaid with geometric designs in colored marble. In front the hall was divided by a low wall into three sections, one containing a sunken basin that was probably used for ritual washing before the service. The back wall was slightly curved and faced east-southeast, in the direction of Jerusalem. Running along this wall was a low platform reached by steps; this may have been the *bimah,* from which the Torah was read. What makes the building unlike any other known to us is a brickwork shrine, approached by steps and with a pair of columns in front, where the Holy Ark was kept. The remains of a Latin inscription tell us that *For the Emperor's health, Mendes [?] Faustos constructed and made at his own expense and placed the Ark for the Holy Torah. . .*

This inscription, coupled with the size and splendor of the building, suggest that in Europe under the Romans, as under the Persian and Moslem rulers to the east, Jews lived in harmony with the governing authorities.

Professor Salo W. Baron suggests* that in Rome, for example, four synagogues were named after four leading Roman individuals. Was it because they wished to place these houses of worship under their powerful protection or was it because these individuals contributed to their erection? However, he also points out that in order not to be too conspicuous they decentralized their worship into thirteen synagogues not as in Alexandria, which boasted a large magnificent edifice.

When, at the end of the nineteenth century, European Jews started to "discover" their "forgotten" brothers in the far-flung iso-

*The Jewish Community, Vol. I, Jewish Publication Society, 1942.

lated communities in China, India and North Africa, they began to learn about their ways of life and how they maintained their identity as Jews. Despite their small numbers, and their isolation and distance from other Jews, they were not obliterated. Had it not been for their synagogues, around which they clustered, and for the Holy Scriptures, which was the "lamp unto their feet," they would have been assimilated and lost forever to Jewry.

With the establishment of the State of Israel most of these Jews settled in Israel. Their ancient communities are now becoming extinct. It behooves us therefore to make a pilgrimage to a scattered number of exotic communities, one or more of which are no more; others are well on the way to extinction. This is the subject of the next chapter.

Mizrach: plaster relief from the Talmudic period

VIII

Exotic Ancient Synagogues in The Near and Far East

Although numerically small, the Jewish community in our country has for centuries enriched our diversity and won the appreciation and regard of other sections of the nation . . . Such were the greetings of Indira Gandhi, the lady Prime Minister of India who came to Cochin in the province of Kerala, India, to celebrate in December, 1968, the 400th anniversary of the erection of the Paradesi which is popularly known as the Cochin Synagogue. In honoring the synagogue, the Prime Minister also noted some 2000 years of the settlement of Jews in that Far East country. The celebration attracted world-wide attention and messages from many lands, including one from President Zalman Shazar of Israel. And the Government of India released a special commemorative stamp in honor of the occasion.

In Cochin the most treasured possession (kept in the Ark) is a precious ancient document incised on copper plates which was given to the Jewish leader Joseph Rabban and his descendants by the native ruler of the province, allegedly in the year 370 C.E. (some maintain this occurred in the eleventh century). It bears the record of a grant of properties and privileges accorded to the Jews for *as long as the moon and the earth shall exist.* This was the first charter granted to the first principality in the Diaspora.

According to an ancient tradition, some seventy to eighty thousand Jewish souls arrived on the coast of Malabar from Majorca

*The quotations on the Cochin Synagogue are drawn from the 400th Anniversary Souvenir Book, 25–Kislev, 5729 (December 15, 1968).

Cochin Synagogue, India

The Ancient Copper Plates

Reading the Torah from the Chair of Moses, Kai-Feng-Fu

where they had been exiled after 70 C.E. Their leader, Joseph Rabban, was of Yemenite origin. Cut off from the Jewish world, these Jews were kept together by the synagogue throughout the various periods of Portuguese, Dutch, British and Indian rule.

In 1968 there were three synagogues—two small ones belonging to the dark-skinned Jews and the main one, called Paradesi, belonging to the white Jews. It was erected in 1568 and is distinguished by having two bimahs (reader's desks)—one on the balcony and the other in the main hall, at the center. The one on the balcony is used for reading the Torah and for conducting the services during the Sabbath and Festivals, while the lower one is for the daily prayers as well as for the mussaf (additional prayer) on the Sabbath and Festivals.

Describing this synagogue, Pierre Loti (1850–1923), famous French novelist, naval officer and renowned world traveler, wrote: *There is perhaps no other synagogue in the world where an ancient style of decoration of an unknown manner is so well preserved.* And Dr. Walter Fischel, world traveler and scholar of Far Eastern Jewry, writes, *Having visited this synagogue in 1959 I can [state] that it could really be called the Taj Mahal* of Indian Jews.*

It is interesting to note that in the seventeenth century when Rabbi Manasseh ben Israel (1604–1657) world Jewish leader, who resided in Amsterdam, petitioned Oliver Cromwell to allow Jews to resettle in England (to which Cromwell informally and tacitly agreed), he cited the Jews in Cochin as an example of how tolerance was extended to his brothers even in far-off India. With the establishment of the State of Israel great numbers have emigrated. After having lived for many years in Jew Town, Cochin, the population of Jews has dwindled from 3000 to 300.

Mrs. Ida Cowen, who has traveled to many remote Jewish communities throughout the world, visited Cochin in 1961 and described the synagogue this way: "Forty feet long, it has two rows of crystal chandeliers and hanging silver lamps. Brass pillars support an upper gallery to which the Scroll of the Law with its golden crown (the gift of a Rajah) is brought from the carved ark for ceremonial reading on Sabbath mornings. Behind the upper gallery, separated from it by

---

*A white marble mausoleum which is a world-renowned architectural gem located at Agra, India.

lattice work, is the women's balcony. Paradesi worshippers face west toward Jerusalem. A striking feature of the synagogue is the floor made of Chinese tiles."*

Kai-Feng-Fu Synagogue in China

Unlike the living community of Cochin Jewry, whose settlement dates back about 1500 years, the ancient Jewry of Kai Feng-Fu in Honan Province of central China is now extinct. Situated on the shores of Whang Ho, or the Yellow River, some 470 miles south of Peking, it probably never numbered more than 300 families or about 1500 souls. The original synagogue, built in 1163, was rebuilt successively; again and again it was inundated as the river overflowed its banks. From various reports we learn that the architecture of the synagogue building, like such structures everywhere, conformed to the architecture of the environment, resembling somewhat a Buddhist temple with Chinese and Hebrew inscriptions. Special features were inscriptions on stone in Chinese and Hebrew; an "elevated Chair of Moses," from which the *Baal Koreh* read the Torah Scroll; the presence of incense burners; a special hall for the worship of dead

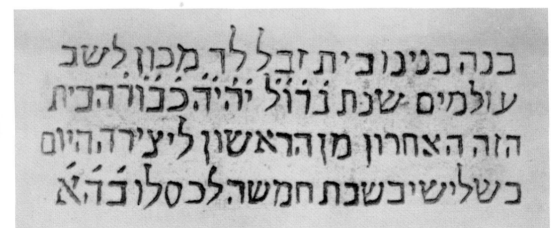

Cochin Hebrew dedicatory inscription on a slab, dated 5102 (1345), from an extinct house of worship

*Ida Cowen, *Jews in the Remote Corners of the World,* chapter on Cochin, Prentice-Hall, Englewood Cliffs, N. J.

ancestors, and a Chinese-Hebrew memorial book of the dead, whose last entries were made in 1670.

It would appear that up to about 200 years ago the Jews of Kai-Feng-Fu, who looked Chinese and wore queues, practiced a religion that combined Judaism, Confucianism, Buddhism and Islam. They observed circumcision, the important Jewish festivals, the Sabbath and the dietary laws. Although they made contact with European Christians in 1605, Western Jewry learned of their existence only in the eighteenth century. They became known to some Christian missionaries in Europe in 1850 after a certain bishop, George Smith, visited China. Two Chinese Protestant Christians whom he sent to the town on a mission of inquiry, reported that the synagogue was partially in ruins, with but a few impoverished Jewish families still living in the neighborhood. The missionaries were told by some local Jews, known as "professors," that "they had nearly starved since their synagogue had been neglected and all but abandoned," but the missionaries were allowed to visit the building. Later they wrote individual reports of their journey to Kai-Feng-Fu, together with a description of the synagogue inscriptions. One of these missionaries stated that anyone known to belong to the Jewish religion was despised and poor; none of the Chinese would associate with Jews, and they were treated as outcasts by the common people. Many who professed Judaism did so in secret, lest they too should be despised. The second of the missionaries reported that the synagogue was in a very bad state. He was informed by a few Jews he encountered that they had no teachers and that within the synagogue there resided only four or five families. He stated that the Jews had three kinds of officers: the rabbi, the prayer leader and the ritual slaughterer to make certain the meat was kosher. Among other things he reported:

> On the days of worship (the Sabbath and festivals), the disciples must all bathe in the place appointed for that purpose, after which they may enter the synagogue. The Rabbi then takes his seat on an elevated platform with a large red satin umbrella held over him. This umbrella is still preserved in the Synagogue. When they bow down to worship, they face the west, (i.e. toward Jerusalem) and in calling upon God, in the Chinese language, they use the word *T'heen* (heaven) and *Tao* (the way). . . . The reason for the neglect of the Jewish religion (in Kai-Feng-Fu) is

because for fifty years there has been no one to instruct them in the knowledge of the . . . Divine classic (the Pentateuch) and in the twenty letters of the Jewish Alphabet.*

From time to time after the publication of Bishop Smith's pamphlet attempts were made to communicate with the Chinese Jews through fellow Jews in Europe, and through Protestant and Catholic missionaries. The first Jew to visit them was one named J.J. Lieberman from Russia, in July 1867. Articles were published in various periodicals. Committees were formed to solicit information, and various steps were taken to get in touch with the lingering survivors of this Jewish colony. For unknown reasons, perhaps because the Chinese feared Westerners and grew increasingly anti-foreign, these attempts failed. Those Jews of the Kai-Feng-Fu community who were not assimilated by the surrounding population left the town for other centers where they could improve their lot and keep in touch with their fellow Jews. As late as the year 1864, a committee of prominent Jewish residents of London arranged for Benjamin II† to visit Kai-Feng-Fu, but unfortunately he died very suddenly on the eve of his departure and the expedition did not take place. The committee subsequently arranged to send some Chinese representatives, but this attempt too proved abortive. According to an account contributed by Mr. D. J. Mills to a periodical entitled *China's Millions* (1891), the partial destruction of the synagogue, noticed by the missionaries sent by Bishop Smith, culminated in the complete wrecking of the buildings about 1856. Mr. Mills remarked: *The destruction of the building began when the poorest among the local Jews started to filch here a stone and there a few bricks. There being no recognized head, this continued until the whole place was demolished, with the few remaining materials being sold to the Moslems. This destruction was completed about thirty-five years ago. One could hardly help weeping at seeing the desolation of this spot where for so many centuries the God of Abraham had been worshiped.* Mr. Mills reported that some two hundred families of Jews were still scattered over the city of Kai-Feng-Fu at this period (1891), although only one family now remained in what had formerly been the Jewish

*The information and quotations are drawn from *Jews in Old China* and *Studies of the Chinese Jews*, edited by Hyman Kublin, Paragon Reprint Corp., 1971.
†A world-renowned Jewish traveler (1818–1864) who emulated the medieval traveler Benjamin of Tudela of the twelfth century.

quarter. *The site of the Temple,* he reported, *is now partly a rubbish heap and partly a pool of water. A stone tablet in the centre serves to preserve the spot as the property of the Jewish community.*

In its heyday the synagogue stood in an open area of some 60,000 square feet surrounded by trees. It was divided by four successive courts, with the synagogue in the center of the fourth court. The other courts contained dwelling houses for the functionaries, a Hall of Ancestors in which the Patriarchs of the Bible—Abraham, Moses, Joshua, Ezra, etc.—were venerated; a special place to build a *sukkah.* Some of the tablets inscribed in Chinese read: *To the Lord of the Religion of Truth and Purity. This religion is in accordance with Heaven, the True.* And in Hebrew the *Shema* and the blessing that follows it (Deuteronomy 6:4–9). Also, *Blessed be the Lord forever. The Lord is God of Gods, a great God.*

Zealous Christian missionaries tried to convert them. Fellow Jews on the other hand, tried to reach them and bring them into the world Jewish community. But unrest, xenophobia and rebellion, which plagued China often, thwarted communications. As late as 1899 they were visited by a Jewish military man of the German army. He stated that his interpreter, having informed him that there were about five hundred Jews left in the town, had introduced him to the "High Priest" who gave him a short resumé of the history of the Jews in China and took him to the site of the former synagogue. He went on to report: *Some 500 feet from the Yellow River embankment we halted before a demolished gate, marking the entrance to a mighty square, covered with grassgrown ruins, pillars, cornices, and colossal chunks of masonry lying singly or in heaps, as if an earthquake or similar natural agency of destruction had shaken a great complex of buildings to pieces.* He reported that the "High Priest" admitted that he knew no Hebrew, *and that the rabbi before him was also innocent of the historic tongue . . . But this inability to read and enjoy the Scriptures did not diminish the good priest's ardour for the perfect preservation of the colony's literary treasures.* Later, the old rabbi removed from a subterranean vault three granite slabs which covered three heavy chests of wood and iron. *There, encased in pieces of thick, soft silk, I saw numerous rolls of papyrus and parchment, the oldest written probably twenty-two or twenty-three centuries ago. I recognized a copy of the Pentateuch, on very large parchment.*

The last page in the history of the famous synagogue of Kai-

Feng-Fu appears to have closed with the announcement in the *Pall Mall Gazette* of February 7, 1913, that the remaining Jewish inhabitants of the town had sold the site of their former synagogue to the "Canadian Mission" and that the transfer of the property had been officially confirmed. The authorities of the Mission were stated to be the custodians of the memorial stones. Eventually the few remaining Jews scattered to Shanghai and Hong Kong, where ultimately they disappeared entirely.

The missionaries brought back the scrolls and prayer books which were no longer used. Several valuable antiquities are today in the possession of the library of the Hebrew Union College in Cincinnati, Ohio. Sometime between 1850 and 1866 the synagogue was destroyed and the few Jews who were left became scattered in China. Early in this century an Anglican bishop, William Charles White, took over the protection of the site. He stayed in the city from 1910 to 1935 and wrote a scientific report on the Jews and the synagogue in a three-volume work entitled *Chinese Jews,* which was published by the University of Toronto Press in 1942.

La Ghriba Synagogue, Djerba, Tunisia

Off the shores of Tunisia in the southern Mediterranean, close to Tripoli (Libya), lies the island of Djerba. Today the Tunisian government is striving to develop the island as the Riviera playground of Tunisia. The chroniclers of Djerba boast of its classical antiquity which they trace from early Greek history. The causeway (Via Zitae), joining Djerba to the mainland, was built by the Romans and regarded as an engineering feat of the highest magnitude. For centuries it was the largest and longest road of this kind in the world. Today Djerba may also be reached by small ferries that ply to and from the mainland.

The Jews of Djerba have lived for many centuries in two villages or ghettos: the *Hara* (ghetto) *Kabira* (big) and *Hara Serira* (little). These villages were centers of Jewish creativity and culture. They housed Jewish printing shops and handicraft shops which manufactured religious objects and books for synagogues and Jewish homes in all of North Africa. They also "exported" rabbis, Cohanim, craftsmen and silversmiths to the neighboring countries. The Jews have lived there for twenty centuries and look just like their Arab neighbors except that at the bottom of their trousers they wear a black

Lag B'Omer night in la Ghriba Synagogue, Djerba, Tunisia
(Photo: David Kidouchim)

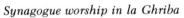

Synagogue worship in la Ghriba

ribbon as a symbol of mourning for the destruction of the Temple. This marks them as members of the Jewish faith. Legend has it that the first settlers were refugees from Zion after the destruction of the First Temple in 586 B.C.E. Indeed Hara Serira was populated until recently by a large number of Cohanim (descendants of the high priest Aaron).* More specifically, they were alleged to have been descendants of the prominent priestly family of Zadok. As in so many legends of this kind, it is told that when their ancestors fled from Jerusalem the Cohanim brought with them a door of the Temple. Around it they built a synagogue, now no longer in existence, which they called *Deleth* (Door). The synagogue which has acquired world-wide fame and has been officially recognized by the Tunisian government as a national shrine and attraction for an annual folk festival is the La Ghriba.

Situated about a mile outside the Hara Serira, this synagogue was built about 100 years ago. It is in open country surrounded by olive groves which abound on the island. It is a large edifice resembling an Islamic mosque and decorated with bright colorful tiles. The exterior looks modest and rather blank. But the interior contains a veritable treasure-trove of sacred, antique furniture and sacred vessels. It is filled with olive-oil lamps dedicated to the memories of the deceased, cedar-wood cupboards and the Holy Ark. But the pride of Djerban Jews are the numerous ornate and valuable Torah Scrolls, silver Torah ornaments, *havdalah* incense-holders, scroll mantles, candlesticks, pointers, beakers and other ceremonial objects.

Ghriba is an Arabic word meaning alien. Legend has it that long ago a mysterious young maiden who settled in Hara Serira was a miracle worker. Her eternal resting place is alleged to be under the Holy Ark. Unique to the La Ghriba synagogue is a large hostel which is built opposite the synagogue. It is a typical caravansary (an inn for camel caravans) common in Moslem countries. The building, constructed around a large yard, offers accommodations in small windowless cubicles to the thousands of pilgrims who flock to the site on Lag B'Omer. The festival, widely publicized by the Tunisian government, attracts Moslems, Christians and Jews from North Africa and

---

*Dr. Nahum Slouchz (1872–1969) scholar and traveler, reported that one of its sons, Rabbi Haim Ha-Cohen Jerbi in Tripoli possessed a genealogical table of his family going back twenty-seven centuries.

Europe. The maimed and crippled, the blind and the deaf, flock to
the La Ghriba for miraculous cures. An all-night vigil is observed and
on Lag B'Omer day a parade is held, led by the synagogue dignitaries
and Tunisian officials who carry the beautiful Torah scrolls from the
La Ghriba to a synagogue nearby.

The various and diverse "honors" related to the Torah scrolls
and the march are auctioned off for "sale" to the highest bidder.
Throughout the night and the next morning, benedictions and prayers are recited by the patriarchs of the synagogue for those who seek
cures and who are in need of succor and healing. Indeed the La
Ghriba festival of Lag B'Omer presents a combination of the celebrations at the Shrine of Rabbi Simon Bar Yohai in Meron (Israel), a
Catholic shrine such as the one at Lourdes (France), and a carnival.
The natives look forward to it the livelong year. Although the rabbis
of Djerba endeavored to reduce its dimensions and even to abolish
it, they did not succeed, for this holiday has long been the largest
source of income and of excitement to the Jewish community.

What the venerable sages of Djerba did not succeed in curbing,
time did. Not so long ago Djerba boasted of a Jewish population of
about 6000. Today it is less than one-twentieth this number. Both
haras, for centuries restricted to Jews, have been overrun by Moslems; the Jews, with some exceptions, have emigrated to Israel. But
the synagogue, its furnishings and ornaments, remain as mute wit-
nesses of a community that proudly bore the appelation "the Jerusalem of North Africa," and attested to scores of generations that kept
the faith.

The Great Synagogue in Baghdad

In 1910 David Solomon Sassoon, renowned bibliophile, orientalist,
distinguished descendant of the world-famous Sassoon family of the
Orient and England, visited Iraq, the home of his ancestors. He
published an account of his journeys in a Hebrew book entitled
Journeys in Babylonia. The book has been reprinted with an introduction and notes and is the source from which we bring this report
of the great synagogue in Baghdad. (In 1949, Solomon D. Sassoon, his
distinguished son, translated and published it in England.)

Jews have lived in Babylonia (now Iraq) more than 2500 years.
In 1948, when the State of Israel was established, a mass emigration
to Israel began. After the Sinai Campaign in 1956, and the Six-Day

War in 1967, there occurred vicious anti-Israel and anti-Jewish persecutions which have destroyed and extinguished the Jewish community, except for a handful of Jewish prisoners. This proud, rich and
influential Jewry is no more. Its Chief Rabbi died in 1971. It is completely isolated from the Jewish world.

Sassoon reports in detail about the synagogues in Baghdad. In
1910 he found thirty-seven houses of worship and described in particular the Slat-li-Kbiri, the Great Synagogue, which in size and history
is the most important. Like other such oriental sanctuaries it, too,
boasted that it was located on the very spot where the exiled King
of Judah, Jehoiachin (597 B.C.E.), erected a sanctuary with materials
brought from the Holy Land. A precis of his report follows:

The synagogue is square in shape. It is divided into twenty-seven
hekhalot, or compartments with sitting accommodation, consisting
of divans made of stone covered with carpets on three sides, leaving
the fourth side open. Fourteen of them were under vaulted archways

Great Synagogue of Baghdad (note uncovered area between the sides and the center)

along the walls, and twelve around the *tevah*,* the reader's desk. The *tevah* is in the center of the synagogue, covered by a roof. The chief *hekhal*, which is in the center on the western wall, contains the holy scrolls. Here also was the seat of honor reserved for the *Nassi* or president (Sassoon), his descendants and their successors. The *hakhmim*, or rabbis, sit on the *tevah*. Under it there is a cupboard to lock away the valuable ritual vessels. Women are seated over the *hekhalot* in galleries behind a lattice-work of wood. If the galleries became too crowded, they overflowed to the roof where they listened to the service.

The Great Synagogue has a rich collection of holy scrolls. In 1910 there were more than seventy. Some of them are enclosed in beautiful cases of gold and silver, others in cases covered with velvet. These scrolls like others in oriental synagogues were dedicated to departed parents and relatives. Or they were dedicated to the prophet Ezekiel or to Ezra the Scribe and so on. Each scroll is named after the donor or honoree.

There is no *Ner Tamid* (Perpetual Lamp) in any of the Baghdad synagogues, but in this one, glass receptacles suspended on chains contain lamps that are kindled by relatives in memory of the deceased. Most oriental synagogues are permeated with the heavy smell of oil from the memorial lamps lit in memory of the departed.

Near the main entrance to the synagogue there is a small stone in the wall which bears the inscription *Even Me-Eretz Yisrael* (a stone from the Land of Israel), which is touched with the fingers and kissed by all who enter and leave the synagogue. Adjoining the Great Synagogue is a large courtyard which is used for worship during the hot season. This division of the synagogue into a winter and summer place of worship was also known to the Babylonian Jews of the Talmudic period. If it rains, straw mats are spread overhead as a cover.

The Ezra Synagogue in Cairo

A synagogue that became world-famous was the so-called Ezra Synagogue in the suburb of Fostat, near Cairo. It achieved universal renown due to the inestimable historical treasures which it preserved throughout a thousand years. Like all ancient synagogues (this

*In Sephardic synagogues the *bimah* is called *tevah* and the ark *hekhal*.

one was 1300 years old) it was overlayed with legends. Alleged to have been originally erected 38 years before the destruction of the Second Temple, it had been called Ezra because it was reputed to contain the Torah scroll which Ezra the Scribe wrote in the fifth century B.C.E. Even Elijah the Prophet was said to have miraculously appeared there.

Legends aside, from the evidence provided by treasures that were found in it, it is quite likely that Maimonides (1135–1204) worshiped in it and that 400 years later the great mystic and saint Isaac Luria—better known as the *Ari* in abbreviation (1534–1572)—studied and worshiped there. These two renowned historical personalities have indeed lent distinction to this synagogue for all time, as have also the priceless treasures found in its *genizah*, as described below. The most complete account of this synagogue was written by Eben-Saphir, a European traveler who published a book of his travels in 1866. The building was a ruin of stone walls and disintegrating wooden ceiling. The two rows of twelve pillars supported stone arches and beams. The Ark containing three scrolls was in the center. The *bimah* was raised. At the right southeast corner was a small cave where Elijah is said to have appeared. At the northeast corner was a small ark believed to have held Ezra's scroll. After much persuasion, the caretaker permitted Eben-Saphir to examine the scroll. He found it to be a very old, worn and rotted parchment written in Sephardic Hebrew script. In the middle of the synagogue was a kind of divan with a canopy. Again according to an old legend, Jeremiah was said to have sat there crosslegged reading his lamentations at the destruction of the First Temple (586 B.C.E.).

The most important place in the synagogue was the hole in the attic behind the women's gallery where lay the old treasures of manuscripts. After much persuasion and bribery Eben-Saphir climbed up and took a number of leaves and papers. Little did he know that he was on the threshold of history. It was Dr. Solomon Schechter, creator of the Jewish Theological Seminary of New York, who later made history and gained immortality by exploring this treasure-trove in 1896–97 and transporting it to the Western world.

Traditional synagogues provide a specific storage place where worn-out prayer books, Bibles, scroll parchments and the like are accumulated and then buried. Containing the Divine Name they are considered sacred and may not be thrown away or placed in waste-disposal receptacles; nor may they be burned. Eventually they are put into a box and buried. The spot selected for their burial must be hallowed ground because they bear the sacred name of God. This place is known as the *Genizah*, or hiding place.

Some 800 to 1000 years ago the old Cairo community was an important center of Jewish life where scholars studied, taught and met at rabbinic gatherings. A century ago many scholars surmised that it contained a large treasure of ancient precious books, parchments and papers depicting Jewish life in the early Middle Ages not only in Egypt but in the Jewish world as a whole. But it remained intact until 1896–97, when Schechter arrived on the scene. As anticipated, he found in the crushed and crowded rubble of the Cairo *Genizah* priceless manuscripts which are now the proud possession of Cambridge University in England, the Jewish Theological Seminary of New York and certain libraries. He worked a full year in that dark hole and brought away thirty boxes filled with parchment pieces and papyri, in all about 100,000 fragments dealing with the Bible, Talmud, philosophy, post-Biblical literature, science, mathematics, medicine and other subjects. They were written in Hebrew and Arabic. The documents, pieces of books and manuscripts were dated from the year 600 to 1000 and shed light on many phases of Jewish life, history and culture. Except for the Dead Sea Scrolls which were discovered some fifty years later, no other recent find was as significant as this one. Hundreds of scholars have worked on this material since their transportation to Europe and America half a century ago. It is estimated that it will take another fifty years to complete the analysis, study, digestion and report on the *Genizah* of the so-called Ezra Synagogue in Fostat.

And now after this excursus to the Near and Far East we return to the Western world to see the dawning of Jewish life in the New World.

IX

Synagogues of the Medieval World: Historic Museums Today

When the Roman legions invaded central and northern Europe the Jews, either as soldiers or as merchants, accompanied the armies. They came up the big Rhone and Rhine rivers and settled along their shores. The oldest definitely proven Jewish community in Germany was Cologne in 331 C. E.

When the Roman empire collapsed and Christianity arrived on the scene with the conversion of Emperor Constantin in the fourth century, their sufferings began. State and Church were now one. The Church taught that the Jews had survived in order to proclaim the living truth of the Christian faith. How? By their humiliation and shame and suffering. Ultimately, it preached, this stiff-necked people would embrace the Church and declare its triumph over Judaism. Thus branded, the Jews became the common prey of willful rulers, of the ignorant rabble, of jealous guilds of craftsmen, of merchants and traders. When it served their own interests, certain rulers protected them. They were the personal property (*servi camerae*) of the barons, bishops and kings to do with as their fancy and notions moved them. The Jews were barred from trades and professions and from owning land. They lived in a constant state of insecurity and danger. Death, exile and homelessness were an ever-present threat. In Germany (and Italy) which was divided and ruled by dukes, bishops and barons, it often happened that Jews exiled from one city or province could find a home in another nearby. Later they would resettle in their previous homes when conditions changed for the better. Not so in England or France, which were united under one rule. When exiled, the Jews had to leave the country altogether, abandoning their homes, synagogues, possessions and wealth behind them to start all over again in another insecure and hateful "home." Permanently locking the synagogue doors was one of the severest punishments inflicted on the Jewish community.

In this life of daily fear, anxiety, suspicion and persecution, disastrous events occurred which added to the profound agony of the times.

The Crusades and the Black Death

The final years of the eleventh century saw the beginning of the First Crusade, a military expedition to recapture the Holy Sepulcher, the place reputed to contain the tomb of Jesus, from the Saracens who were the rulers of Palestine. Some of the knights and pilgrims who joined the Crusades were devout men; others were mere adventurers; and many, an ignorant rabble of fanatics. To arouse their enthusiasm and win recruits, fiery sermons were preached against the "infidels." As a result, in many places—though not all—it became not only respectable but actually a pious duty preliminary to the Holy Crusade to rob and kill the infidels who were near at hand, the Jews.

In the Rhine Valley, until then a center of Jewish life and culture, the slaughter began in the spring of 1096 and continued for three months. In Mainz, 1300 Jews were killed. In Worms the bishop opened the doors of the cathedral to 800 Jews who managed to crowd inside; all the rest were slaughtered. It is said that during that bloody spring, as many as 12,000 Jews perished in the Rhine Valley alone. As time went on, crusade followed crusade. Certain bishops voiced pleas for Christian compassion. But in the twelfth century, Peter of Cluny, head of a great abbey, called for the destruction of the Jews. In 1215, Pope Innocent III convened the Fourth Lateran Council which issued a cruel edict. Not only were Jews forbidden to hold public office or to hire Christian servants; from then on they were required to wear a special yellow patch or cap proclaiming who they were. Thus, like Cain of old, they were "branded," shunned, and made conspicuous targets of persecution—as were their descendants many years later when, under the Nazi rule, they were forced to wear the Jewish star.

Even this outrage was not all; their sacred books too were not spared. In Paris in the summer of 1242, twenty-four cartloads of

Talmudic literature were publicly burned. At Rottingen, there was an uprising in 1298 in which the whole Jewish community was burned at the stake. In Breslau, a Christian chapel was built with Jewish money after nearly the entire Jewish community had been wiped out. Then, in 1290, the Jews were expelled from England; in 1306 they were expelled from France; in 1336 renewed persecution began in Germany. Thus, the disasters mounted and gained momentum.

If all these sufferings and horrors can be said to have reached a climax, it came about halfway through the fourteenth century when the Black Death, an epidemic resembling the bubonic plague, swept through Europe, killing from a third to a half of the general population. Although Jews were among its countless victims, the Christians superstitiously blamed them. They, the Jews, were held responsible for this calamity. The terror-stricken populace accused the Jews of poisoning the wells and rivers. As a result, there were wholesale massacres and forced baptisms; many Jews faced with the choice of the one or the other, committed suicide. More than two hundred Jewish communities in Germany were exterminated. It was the greatest disaster that German Jewry experienced up to the Nazi holocaust. Jewish learning came to a near-stop as schools closed down. Superstition flourished. Echoes of these tragic events are found in the prayer book. One of the best-known dirges is *Av Harahamim*, "Father of Mercy," which is recited on most Sabbath mornings in the Ashkenazic synagogues.

Summarizing in an overview of medieval Jewish life, Leopold Zunz (1794–1886), the German Jewish scholar and historian wrote: *If there are ranks in suffering, Israel takes precedence of all the nations; if the duration of sorrows and the patience with which they were borne ennoble, the Jews can challenge the aristocracy of every land; if a literature is called rich in the possession of a few classical tragedies, what shall we say to a National Tragedy in which the poets and the actors were also the heroes?*

The Synagogues in Northern Europe: Worms

In such a setting, the remarkable thing is that the Jews or the synagogue managed to survive at all. Of the relatively few synagogue buildings that did outlive this medieval disaster, the earliest in Northern Europe was at Worms, the Rhineland city, one of whose sons, Rabbi Meir of Rothenburg, was the outstanding scholar and leader of European Jewry. (See below.) Its synagogue had been started in 1034 and rebuilt at the end of the twelfth century. It was small, rectangular in shape, very simple, and contained one door placed at the side and not fronting the street in order to avoid being conspicuous or drawing attention. Despite the ravages of time and repeated persecution, it survived with little change until the savage pogrom of November 9, 1938, when it was burned down by the Nazis. The stone frame of the flame-blackened Holy Ark remained standing. The Torah scrolls, which had withstood the fire, were destroyed by explosives. The historic scroll written by Rabbi Meir of Rothenburg (see page 104) while he was imprisoned was among them. The Rashi Chapel (see below) was destroyed. Precious ornaments, ancient manuscripts, incunabula, historical records (many synagogues preserved invaluable historical and documentary records) and books were all wantonly destroyed. But the shell of the building remained standing. After the war the German government rebuilt it in a kind of replica, to serve as a museum or showplace.

As in other times and places, the architecture of the synagogue at Worms reflected the church buildings around it. Those of ancient Palestine had followed the plan of the Roman basilica, which had a flat roof supported by pillars and a central nave or hall. The one at Worms followed the Romanesque style that prevailed in Europe during the early part of the Middle Ages—that is, it had a floor-plan similar to that of the basilica but the pillars supported a ceiling that was vaulted to form rounded arches overhead. The two columns in the middle supported the vaulted ceiling dividing the space into two aisles rather than three. The low ceiling and small room gave a feeling of warmth and intimacy.

Perhaps the chief explanation for the two aisles rather than three was the connection between the number three and the Christian Trinity, and the wish to avoid one more painful reminder of the hostile world outside. The *bimah* or *almemar*, the elevated reading platform from which the Scripture was read, was placed in the center so as to dominate the space between the two columns. Inscribed on one of the columns and on the walls were the names of the donors and of the Jewish artists who had designed the interior. These were preserved through more than eight centuries until the night in

Rashi Chapel, Worms

Interior of synagogue in Worms

November 1938 when the unprecedented Nazi atrocities destroyed them forever.

Originally the synagogue at Worms appears to have been attended by men only; at any rate, there was no women's section until one was added in 1213. Meanwhile, the building had been expanded to include a room for study, known as the Rashi Chapel in honor of the most renowned scholar who had studied there for a while.

One of the striking oddities of the synagogue was the presence of two perpetual lamps instead of the one which is found in all houses of worship. They were to eternize the memories of two anonymous martyrs who heroically gave their lives to save the community from total destruction as a result of a ritual accusation to which the two innocents "confessed." In addition to this symbol, a special memorial prayer was recited through the centuries in their honor on the last day of Passover, the day of their martyrdom.

Prague: Synagogue, Cemetery and Museum

About 200 miles to the east of Worms is Prague, the capital of what is now Czechoslovakia. It was once the home of one of the oldest Jewish communities in Europe. Among the historic sights of Prague are its synagogue and the cemetery which is nearby, close to the center of the Old Town. This cemetery is of special interest. In many places Jewish law forbade removing a body from a grave for any reason, even to make way for a later burial. Thus, in Prague as in other old communities, when no more space was obtainable in the cemetery, a new layer of soil was brought in to cover the old, and new graves were dug in that layer. At the same time, the headstones from the graves underneath were brought up to the new level. Through the centuries the process was repeated several times, until the cemetery became a forest of weatherbeaten tombstones, so closely packed together as to be almost impossible to count. Just how many there are no one knows but they are estimated to number as many as twenty thousand. This cemetery (as others) has rightfully been called a "chronicle in stone." Among the noted Jews buried there are the semi-legendary Rabbi Judah Loew (1520–1609), known as a worker of miracles and creator of the *Golem*—a homunculus molded out of clay—and the historian, astronomer and mathematician David Gans (1541–1613). Rabbi Loew, known as the Maharal, is commemorated as well by a statue still standing in front of the Prague City Hall.

Old—New Synagogue in Prague (Photo: Vladimir Soukop)

The Prague Altneuschul was long spoken of as the second oldest synagogue in Europe. Although there is uncertainty about just when the original synagogue was built, it is believed to date back to the late eleventh century, and to have been renovated around the middle of the twelfth. It was said that after the Easter Sunday pogrom of 1389* the rabbis forbade any further renovations because the building was hallowed by the blood of the martyrs which had been shed on that spot and should therefore not be profaned by cement, lime and paint. Nevertheless, it has since been almost entirely rebuilt after having been partly burned and demolished by the rioting mobs. The building thus rebuilt several times is most probably the origin of the name *Altneuschul*—which means literally "Old-New Synagogue." A more romantic explanation is provided by the legend that its foundation consisted of stones salvaged from the ruins of the Temple after its destruction in the year 70, and was brought from the Holy Land by Jewish exiles who vowed that when the Messiah came they would demolish the synagogue and once again return the stones to Mount Zion. According to this explanation the synagogue took its name from the words *al t'nay*, which in Hebrew mean "on condition."

In its small size and rectangular shape, divided by pillars into two aisles, the present building resembles the synagogue at Worms. But in style it is Gothic, rather than Romanesque, with thin, tall columns and pointed rather than round arches overhead. Here, too, the women's section is on the same floor but in an adjoining room. The *Aron Kodesh*, the Holy Ark, stands at the eastern wall. The pulpit, enclosed by a grille of wrought iron, stands in the center of the room, and the *amud*, or lectern, from which the cantor leads the service is at a lower level than the rest. This was usual in the medieval synagogue and gave poignant expression to the words of the Psalmist (130:1) with which the service began: *Out of the depths I call unto Thee, O Lord.*

In 1939 the Nazis overran Prague and not long thereafter convoys began to leave for Theresienstadt, Auschwitz, Birkenau and other death camps. While the Jews were being exterminated the Nazis conceived the idea of erecting a vast museum to house all religious, cultural and art objects of all synagogues and institutions in

---

*It occurred when the procession of the host (the consecrated bread and wine used in the Easter Service) passed through the Jewish street. Jewish children playing with sand accidentally besprinkled it. Three thousand Jews were slain by the mob.

Pinkas Synagogue in Prague (note the list of the Nazi concentration and death camps) (Photo: Vladimir Soukop)

the Czech lands. The Jews were forced to build this museum as slave laborers. The collection grew and soon overflowed into the Prague synagogues.

When Hitler's "thousand-year" Third Reich was defeated, the idea of the Prague Jewish Museum was fostered, organized and completed. Today the Czech Communist government has made it part of the national state museums. The museum has some 4,000 Torah scrolls, 6,000 silver Torah-breastplates, 2,000 *parokhot*, or Torah curtains of heavy silk, velvet or brocade, and tens of thousands of other ceremonial and secular objects depicting Jewish life in the once-proud lands of Bohemia and Moravia. Most heartrending are the names of 77,297 unburied victims killed in the seven-year terror and inscribed on the walls of the Pinkas synagogue near the Altneuschul. The famous age-old synagogues of Prague are part of this museum. And, may it be said to the credit of the State Museum, it has been publishing beautiful, colorful books such as the *The Prague Ghetto, The Old Prague Jewish Cemetery, The Pinkas Synagogue* and others, preserving the monuments and documents of the past, and revealing the rich cultural religious and artistic creativity of a world that is no more.

Synagogues in Toledo, Spain

In many ways the synagogues of medieval Spain provide a striking contrast to those in other parts of Europe. As indicated, because of the insecurity of the Jews in the north, their synagogue buildings were inconspicuous and the sacred vessels simple. But in Spain they reflect the very different kind of life which the Jews there led for hundreds of years. There had been Jewish colonies in Spain at least since the third century; and after it was conquered by the Moslems in 711, the Jews prospered as bankers, physicians, statesmen and landowners. By the tenth century, in such cities as Toledo, Cordova, Seville and Lucena there were Jewish academies that often overshadowed those of the East as centers of learning. But they too underwent periods of persecution. During the eleventh century, Crusaders from the north drove the Moslems out of Toledo for a while. During the twelfth century, Moslems of a fanatical sect known as the Almohades arrived from North Africa and began burning synagogues with the same zeal as had been shown by Christians in other parts of Europe. It was because of the Almohades that the great

Abulafia Synagogue or Great Synagogue, Toledo, Spain

Jewish physician and philosopher Moses Maimonides fled to Egypt from Cordova, where he was born in 1135.

The kingdom of Castile, to the north of Cordova, escaped the invasion of the Almohades. In Toledo, its capital, refugees from the south were welcomed, and as a result Toledo soon became the chief center of Jewish life in Spain. It was here, during the days of relative peace and prosperity, that two of the finest surviving monuments to medieval Judaism were built. The older and larger, known as the Great Synagogue, dates to the last years of the twelfth century. Standing in the heart of what was then the Jewish quarter, it has a modest appearance in keeping with its surroundings. When you step inside the outer gate, a pleasant surprise awaits you. You find yourself in a garden fragrant with roses and acacias, with a fountain in one corner and a cypress-lined walk leading to the doorway of the synagogue itself. Inside, all is lightness and grace—an example of the Moorish style of architecture that prevailed in Spain after the Islamic conquest. A rectangular wall, measuring about seventy by ninety feet, is divided into five arcades by rows of octagonal columns surmounted by carved capitals. Everywhere overhead—lining the horseshoe arches, the frieze above them, and the paneled ceiling—are geometrical patterns, medallions, rosettes, and fleurs-de-lys,* interwoven with the Shield of David.

A century before the building of the Great Synagogue, Pope Gregory VII had issued his edict forbidding Christians to employ Jews. The rulers of Castile, however, not only made them welcome but continued to ignore the ban for many years. King Pedro I, who came to the throne in 1350, hired Jews as tax collectors and even made one of the richest of them, Samuel HaLevi Abulafia, his treasurer and right-hand man. Abulafia's career ended tragically when Pedro—whose capricious behavior earned him the nickname of "The Cruel"—had him executed on a false accusation of treason. But Samuel Abulafia did leave behind him a beautiful monument—a synagogue he had financed and built. It was to preserve his name for generations to come.

The Abulafia synagogue is somewhat smaller than the Great Synagogue, measuring about thirty by seventy-five feet. It has no central pillars; instead, its outer walls are lined with fifty-four arcades, borne on double columns of alabaster. Underneath the ar-

*A three-petal floral design.

cades, delicate lattices carved from the same alabaster, all differing from one another, let in a diffused light. Everywhere, once again, are stylized designs showing the influence of Islam, whose followers, like the Jews, were forbidden by their religion to use animal or human forms. Underneath the windows, alternating with these designs, are verses from the Psalms in Hebrew lettering that is one of the loveliest examples of its kind. Overhead, the high ceiling is of Lebanon cedar inlaid with mother-of-pearl. The women's gallery is screened off by a lattice of carved alabaster, and its walls are appropriately ornamented with the verses from the Song of Miriam in Exodus 15.

On the eastern wall of the Abulafia synagogue is the niche where the *Aron Kodesh* once stood. But, although it still carries the date and the names of the donors, the niche has long been empty. Instead of the Holy Ark, there is now a Christian altar; crucifixes and images of saints line its walls. It is now known as El Transito, a name that refers to the death and burial of Jesus. The Great Synagogue met the same fate; it is now the church of Santa Maria de la Blanca. Behind this transformation, once again, is a terrible story of gathering hatred and persecution. In Castile, even while its Jewish communities continued to flourish, the same tide that had overwhelmed the rest of Europe was slowly rising. And though its coming had been delayed, the persecution that overtook the Jews of Spain was in many ways more dreadful than anything that had preceded it.

The Marranos: Inquisition and Expulsion

It began on Ash Wednesday, March 15, 1391, with riots in Seville that left the Jewish quarter in ruins and two thousand of its people dead. This time even Toledo did not escape. It is said that the worst violence there took place on the 9th of Av—a grim reminder of the fall of Jerusalem many centuries ago. That year saw the beginning of a wholesale conversion of the Jews. Thenceforward, three times a year, every synagogue was visited by a Dominican monk who exhorted the congregation to renounce the Jewish faith and submit to baptism. The leader in this campaign was a Dominican friar, Vincente Ferrer (1350–1419), who traveled through Spain with a cross in one hand and the Torah in the other, followed by flagellants* calling on Jews to convert or die. He so terrified his hearers that he was able to boast

*Fanatics who lash and lacerate themselves with thongs and chains.

of being personally responsible for the "rescue," i. e., conversion of 35,000 Jews.

Robert Browning (1812–1889), outstanding English poet, describes in his poem, *Holy Cross Day,* (an annual event when Jews were compelled to attend Christian services in Rome), the scene of Jews being forced to listen to "conversion sermons." We quote one stanza of the listeners' comments:

> Higgledy piggledy, packed we lie
> Rats in a hamper, swine in a stye,
> Wasps in a bottle, frogs in a sieve,
> Worms in a carcass, fleas in a sleeve,
> Hist! Square shoulders, settle your thumbs
> And buzz for the bishop—here he comes.

Because of these wholesale conversions, Spanish and Jewish history became intertwined in a peculiar way. Many of the converts took advantage of their new status and married into the aristocracy, thus consolidating the rank they had already achieved as persons of wealth and high position. But at the same time, the new converts were hated and despised by many people. They were called Marranos—a word said to mean "the damned" or "the swine." Many of the clergy suspected that these converts were still Jews at heart, and that they continued to practice their old religion in secret.

It soon became clear that forced conversion, far from solving their personal problem, had only made things worse for the Marranos. Nowhere was this clearer than in Toledo, where most of the tax-gatherers were Marranos. In 1449, when they were sent to collect a special levy for the defense of the city, they were assaulted by the populace, who resented the tax just as they resented the Marranos themselves. Their houses were destroyed and those who resisted were beaten or killed. It was after this outbreak that the king of Castile finally issued an edict of his own, forbidding new Christians to hold public office.

This did not, however, stop the rioting and persecution which broke out again and again in Toledo and elsewhere. And when in 1480 the Inquisition came to Spain, the fate of Jews and Marranos alike was sealed.

The ruler of Castile in this era was Queen Isabella, whose marriage to Ferdinand of Aragon in northeast Spain had united the two kingdoms. Isabella was a pious woman, and when her confessor, Tomás de Torquemada, urged her to bring the Inquisition to her country, she finally agreed. Begun in southern France, the Inquisition consisted of questioning suspected heretics, under the threat of torture, in order to bring them back into the Christian fold. Those who refused to recant were as a rule sentenced to death by burning at the stake. But nowhere in Europe was the Inquisition more cruel or more thorough than in Spain under Torquemada (1420–1498). The first execution took place there in 1481. After that, it was only a matter of time before life for both Jews and Marranos in Spain became impossible. On March 31, 1492, the Spanish rulers did what the English and the French before them had done. They ordered all Jews to leave the country within four months or be put to death.

So bitter were the Jews about their exile from Spain that later generations refrained from returning to settle there. It was not until the last three decades in the twentieth century that they have begun to return inconspicuously in small numbers. At present the Jewish community numbers about 7000 souls, or .05 percent of the total population. The climate has become more favorable; synagogues now exist in Madrid and Barcelona. The first religious service in modern Spain was held in Cordova, in 1935, on the occasion of the 800th anniversary of Moses Ben Maimon, better known as Maimonides. Near the Cordova Synagogue—now a national monument— the Spanish government erected a statue of the renowned Jewish philosopher, and named the square Piaza Maimonides. Furthermore, in 1971 the government declared the Toledo synagogues national monuments.

It is now nearly 500 years since the Jews left Spain, but their imprint and legacy still exist. It is not uncommon for practicing Catholics to have Spanish-Jewish family names such as Levy, Benjamin and the like. In the large cities certain street names as well as Jewish sections and Jewish landmarks still evoke forgotten memories.

Before they were converted into churches (and thus saved), the synagogues of Toledo had been subjected to indignities and defilement. Many European synagogues experienced the same fate, as for example the one in Trani, Italy, now called St. Anna. In Segovia, the Church of Corpus Christi was formerly a great synagogue. The search for buildings that had been former synagogues is continuing.

In 1966 a young scholar by the name of Don A. Halperin, son of an architect who designed several American synagogues, traveled through the Iberian peninsula doing research on this subject. He describes two finds in northern and central Spain which are now churches. (We shall return to the martyrdom of the synagogue in Chapter XIV.)

Survival through the Synagogue

The story of what became of the Jews of Spain after their expulsion —where they went, and how the survivors began life anew—will be told in the following chapter. But here we may note that their history, and that of the Jews elsewhere in medieval Europe, well illustrates how important the synagogue continued to be as the center of Jewish life. Their exile and suffering were forcibly brought to their attention by an unplastered or unpainted spot on the synagogue wall. Without the synagogue as their pillar of strength, it is unlikely that the Jews of Europe could have survived as a people. For the synagogue was literally all they had. Refugees, who were left homeless after a pogrom, had no recourse or shelter except the synagogue in whatever town they could enter as they fled the rioting mobs. Never had the practice of *tzedakah* been more necessary for the survival of their own people. Funds collected for the needy were put into a general fund known as the *kuppah*, or chest. According to Maimonides, every Jewish community consisting of ten or more people had its own *kuppah*. The trustees of the fund were respected members of the congregation who were known as *Gabbaim*. They collected contributions every day and distributed them each week on the day before the Sabbath or festival. Usually the courtyard of the synagogue contained some lodging accommodations for wayfarers. These were, no doubt, filled again and again to overflowing by Jews who escaped the rioting of mobs and the pillaging of their homes.

In addition to the function it had in such times of crisis, the synagogue likewise continued to be the center through which the Jews of the community kept in touch with the outside world and through which they governed themselves. In a sense, it became a court of law as well as a center of worship and of learning. Here were kept community funds and possibly private funds. Here was a kind of employment agency, the depository of communal and private records, an archive of historical documents and the like.

In some European countries, notably France and Germany, it became accepted custom that any Jew could bring the Sabbath service to a halt if he had a grievance against a member or an organization of the community. Since every Jew attended the daily service, public opinion could thus be aroused. It is easy to see that this very democratic procedure, if abused, could make orderly worship impossible. Consequently, the rabbis established various limiting rules, known as *takkanot* (regulations). One such *takkanah* (regulation), enacted by Rabbi Gershom of Mainz (965–1028), widely known as *Light of the Diaspora*, permitted this right to be exercised at the Sabbath service only after the complaint had three times been made public during a weekday service.

Another *takkanah* for which Rabbi Gershom was responsible had to do with lost articles whose loss was announced in the synagogue. It provided that anyone who had suffered a loss could publicly declare a *herem* (excommunication decree) to compel whoever knew the identity of the finder to make that information public at once. Yet another was the *takkanah* that forbade the exclusion of any Jew from prayer in a synagogue which happened to be privately financed. In Italy too a rabbi formulated a *takkanah* which limited the right of assembly in any place other than the synagogue to six persons. The purpose of this, of course, was to prevent arousing the suspicion of non-Jews in the surrounding population. How much suspicion any such gathering can arouse is suggested by the regulation enforced centuries later by fascist military governments, making it a crime for more than five persons to assemble in a private home.

Another practice connected with the synagogue that strikes a contemporary note was the ransoming of captives. The wealth of certain Jews made them a target for kidnaping; the kinship and ties of Jews to one another—the poor no less than the rich—were exploited by pirates and rulers alike. A center for pirates was the island of Malta in the Mediterranean Sea, seat of the so-called Knights of St. John, who "distinguished" themselves by preying on sea travelers. Their victims were merchants, Jewish pilgrims to the Holy Land and others. Those not ransomed were made slaves. (There was in Malta a community of Jewish slaves who had not been redeemed, which had its own synagogue and burial grounds.*) Pirates also operated off

*"A Community of Slaves," by Cecil Roth, in *Personalities and Events in Jewish History*, Jewish Publication Society, 1953.

the Barbary Coast of Africa. To pay the ransom, they asked Jewish communities, particularly in the Mediterranean region, to arrange for special organizations and funds to raise the needed amount. Venetian Jewry was a world center for the ransoming of captive Jews and for the rescue of their brothers who were in distressed circumstances.

But it was not only pirates who held prisoners for ransom. In 1286 Emperor Rudolf boldly imprisoned Rabbi Meir of Rothenburg (1220–1293), the greatest rabbinic scholar of his generation, for attempting to emigrate to the Holy Land. Rudolf demanded an exorbitant sum. But the saintly rabbi, who was then nearly seventy, refused to let himself be ransomed lest other rulers also adopt the cruel practice of blackmail. Like Rabbi Akiba, who was imprisoned by the Romans eleven centuries earlier, Rabbi Meir spent seven years in a dingy cell and—without his library of manuscripts—served his people by answering *sh'elot* (questions on Law) directed to him, as well as writing a Torah scroll, and thus continued to minister to his people to the end. And so he died in prison. It was not until fourteen years after his death that his body was ransomed so that it could be given proper Jewish burial. Rabbi Alexander Susskind of Frankfurt, who paid the ransom, requested that his reward be burial beside Rabbi Meir's grave. This melancholy episode was only one in the all but endless chronicle of indignities that were the lot of Jews in medieval Europe. It was Rabbi Meir himself who commemorated another calamity of the year 1240: the public burning of wagonloads of handwritten Talmudic books (printing had not been invented yet) in the city square of Paris. His poem is still recited in the synagogue on the Fast Day, the Ninth of Av, which memorializes the fall of Jerusalem and the destruction of the First and Second Temples. He declares mournfully (we quote only three stanzas):

> And thou (the Law) revealed amid a heavenly fire,
> By earthly fire consumed,
> Say how the foe unscratched escaped the pyre
> Thy flames illumed.
>
> *
>
> Moses and Aaron in the mountain Hor,
> I will of them inquire:
> Is there another to replace this Law
> Devoured of fire?

*

I am astonished that the day's fair light
Yet shineth brilliantly
On all things:—it is ever dark as night
To me and thee.

(Translated by Nina Davis)

About the time the exiles from Spain found safe havens in Amsterdam, London, and the New World, western Europe began to emerge from the medieval night into the dawn of the modern era. A more tolerant spirit began to prevail, and as soon as the wanderers began to strike roots in their new homes they started to erect houses of worship, modeled after those they had left in Spain. We now approach the threshold of modern times, the Emancipation Movement, and the settlement of a brave new world.

Funeral procession in old Prague—note the dead body wrapped in a shroud and the tzeḍakah collection box

X

The Synagogue at the Threshold of Modern Times: Holland, England and Poland

Exiles from Spain

It is estimated that the number of Jews who left Spain in the fateful year 1492 totaled about 200,000. Where did these fleeing thousands go? France admitted only converted Jews coming as Christians. Approximately 100,000 to 120,000 emigrated to Portugal, where they were allowed to remain for a time. About 50,000 sailed to cities in North Africa, Italy and the East, especially Turkey where they were welcome. Many who landed in Africa wandered into the desert and starved; some were taken captive and sold into slavery; but a hardy few managed to survive.

In certain parts of Italy, things were better. Jewish refugees who landed at such places as Naples, Salerno, Ferrara, and Venice were welcomed by their brethren. Since the government allowed them to remain, they were even treated well, at least for a while. But the sixteenth century brought the reaction of the Catholic Church against the Protestant Reformation, set off by Martin Luther, and this Counter Reformation brought new restrictions for the Jews. Often this meant a restriction on the number of families permitted to reside in any given place. As a result, by the close of the sixteenth century no city in Italy had more than two thousand Jewish inhabitants. Small communities persisted in such places as Siena, where Jews had lived since the Middle Ages, and whose synagogue, one of the oldest, is still standing in Italy. Other such communities were found in Mantua, Padua, and Correggio. Even in a few very small towns—such as San Daniele del Friuli in the north, or Conegliano Veneto, near Venice, or Sermide, not far from Mantua, Jewish builder-craftsmen erected some splendidly decorated houses of worship.

As stated, the majority of those who fled from the Spanish Inquisition found their way across the border into Portugal. Here, once again, only small groups were able to remain for very long, and then only by going through the motion of accepting baptism. In secret they continued to worship as Jews; some of their descendants live there as Marranos even today.

But for others, Portugal was only a way station in their search for a refuge from persecution. For some time, small numbers of Jews had been finding their way from Spain to the cities of Holland and Flanders (now in Belgium and France). During most of the sixteenth century, the Low Countries had been under the domination of Spain; but in 1588 the Spanish Armada was defeated by British naval forces, and the Dutch became independent. Five years later, in 1593, a group of Marranos arrived in Amsterdam, where they continued to worship secretly as they had done in Portugal. On Yom Kippur 1597, their services were interrupted by a group of neighbors whose suspicions had been aroused. Remembering the hated rule of Catholic Spain, they had taken the mysterious foreigners for Catholics! On being told that these were in fact secret Jews, the city authorities gave them permission to remain. A year later, in 1598, there was rejoicing in Amsterdam as a synagogue was publicly dedicated.

From then on, the Jewish colony in Amsterdam grew rapidly; early in the seventeenth century it included more than five hundred families. Among those were not a few Marranos who had been received back into the Jewish faith. It is said that in the course of a very few years the rabbi of Amsterdam reinstated no less than 250 converted Jews.

Excommunication in the Synagogue

Among the reinstated was a man named Uriel da Costa (1585–1640), who arrived in Amsterdam some time between 1612 and 1615. Born in Portugal of a Marrano family, he had been a practicing Catholic, a student of church law, and the treasurer of a Christian congregation. After being received into the synagogue, shortly after his arrival, it became evident that he was not wholly reconciled to his ancestral faith. He published a book, *Proposals Against Tradition,* which in 1618 led to his excommunication by the rabbinical bodies of Hamburg, Venice and Amsterdam. The synagogue as the center of religious, social and community life would not countenance religious heresies because its very existence was threatened and its congregants were already barely tolerated by their Christian neighbors.

Indeed da Costa's repudiation of the traditional beliefs in immortality, resurrection, divine reward and punishment aroused the anger of the Church because they were heretical. The Dutch courts ordered his books to be confiscated and destroyed; the Jewish community if only in self-defense had to take action against him.

The pronouncement of excommunication took place in the synagogue, and few moments can have been more awesome than those during which black candles were extinguished one by one, and the silence was broken by a final blast from the *shofar*. For the tormented Uriel da Costa, this ceremony took place not once but twice. Fifteen years later, he again recanted his heresy and was again admitted to the synagogue. But his restless criticisms were soon renewed and this time they were even more extreme. Once more the black candles were ceremoniously put out and the notes of the *shofar* pronounced him excommunicated. When he petitioned a third time for permission to worship as a Jew, it was granted only after he had accepted the punishment of being publicly whipped in the synagogue. The burden of this final humiliation was more than the unfortunate Uriel could bear, and he killed himself.

In 1655 the Jewish Community of Amsterdam saw the excommunication of a twenty-three-year-old heretic, Baruch (or Benedict) Spinoza, (1632–1677). Also a descendant of Marranos, he was born in Holland of Sephardic parents. Spinoza wrote in Latin, and his fellow-Jews, fearing the effect of his heretical opinions in the Christian world, disavowed him. Unlike Uriel, he never again entered a synagogue or had any contact with his own people. He never recanted his belief that angels were non-existent, nor his criticisms of the Bible, nor his rejection of the faith in the Revelation at Sinai. But because of the beauty and simplicity of his character, and the profound influence of his writings on subsequent philosophy, many leading Jews through the centuries have urged that his excommunication be revoked posthumously. And even though this has never formally occurred, Spinoza continues to be regarded as a Jewish philosopher whose thinking was influenced by medieval Jewish philosophers such as Maimonides.

Holy Ark of Spanish and Portugese Synagogue, Amsterdam

Two Venetian Synagogues

The Portuguese Synagogue at Amsterdam

Such defections as those of Spinoza and Uriel da Costa were, however, the exception in Amsterdam, which soon came to be known as
the Dutch Jerusalem. A warmly vivid picture of the Jewish quarter
in Amsterdam has come down to us in the work of the celebrated
painter Rembrandt (1606–1669), who made his home in the Jewish
quarter for many years. Himself a Protestant, he drew repeatedly on
the scenes around him for his depiction of Biblical subjects, often
finding inspiration in the figures of the poor and the aged among his
Jewish neighbors. Of his two hundred portraits of men, some thirty-
seven were Jews. He also painted Manasseh ben Israel (see page 74)
and other Jewish dignitaries.

There were many wealthy and conscientious Jews especially
among the Marranos, who had left Spain and Portugal and now
longed to practice their faith openly. In April 1671, the four corner-
stones were laid in Amsterdam for a new and splendid synagogue
which was made possible by the merging of three separate congregations into one. It was destined to become the model for such buildings elsewhere, especially in England and the New World. When it
was completed after two years' work, the ceremonies of dedication
lasted six days and were an occasion for the greatest rejoicing. Down
to the present day, the Portuguese synagogue in Amsterdam remains
a landmark for visitors, Jews and non-Jews alike.

Remembering the elaborate, beautiful double rows of columns
supporting the balconies for the women worshipers in the Toledo
and other Spanish synagogues, the Portuguese Jews in Amsterdam
modeled their new synagogue after the Moorish architectural style
of their old home.

Measuring 125 by 95 feet, the building is three stories high. Its
main hall seats 1227 men, and in the galleries above it there is space
for 400 women. The roof is supported by twelve mammoth columns,
symbolizing the twelve tribes of Israel. There are seventy-two (6x12)
windows. During services the hall glimmers with the light of hundreds of candles reputed to number 613, one for each of the Mosaic
Commandments. The raised *bimah*, built of Brazilian rosewood,
stands in the center towards the rear of the hall, and the monumental
Ark, crowned with two tablets of the Law, fills almost the entire
eastern wall. Its fortress-like outer design is reminiscent of the ancient Temple of Solomon, and was drawn from a wooden model

made by a Jew in Amsterdam earlier in the same century. Scenes of the synagogue have been recorded for posterity by a French non-Jewish artist, Bernar Picart (1673–1733), whose vivid engravings of the religious ceremonies in it have appeared in numerous editions and to this day adorn many Jewish homes and institutions.

The prestige attained by the Sephardic colony in Amsterdam was partly the result of the wealth and culture of its leaders. One of the four congregants who took part in laying the synagogue's corner-stones had been—like Samuel Abulafia in the Castile of a happier day —the financial agent of the king of Portugal and remained his financial adviser even in exile. Others had come to wealth and prominence through international trade. Their relations with the Christian community were so cordial that a number of non-Jews contributed to the building fund.

Bevis Marks Synagogue, London

It was not only in Amsterdam that such colonies flourished during the seventeenth century. In 1622 Denmark opened its doors to the Jews. And in 1657, after a ban lasting four hundred years, Jews were once again permitted to live in England. Within two years, in 1659, the first synagogue since the early Middle Ages was established in London by a newly arrived group of Sephardic Jews. For some years they met in a small building in Creechurch Lane. In 1699 they took a sixty-one-year lease on a plot of land at Plough Yard for the construction of what has been known ever since as the Bevis Marks Synagogue, named after the street in central London where it stands to this day.

Completed and dedicated in 1702, and reconstructed after a fire in 1749, the building measures eighty by fifty feet. Its interior is much like that of the Portuguese synagogue at Amsterdam. In the ceiling supported by its twelve columns is a beam from a royal ship presented by Queen Anne of England to her loyal subjects.

For more than a century the Bevis Marks Synagogue was the chief center of English Jewry. It kept in close touch with its two Sephardic sister congregations in Amsterdam and in the Italian city of Livorno. At one time—although nothing came of the project—its leaders negotiated to acquire land in the American colonies of Georgia and Carolina so that poor Jews might emigrate to begin life anew in the New World. Jewish communities that had been established on the Caribbean islands of Jamaica and Barbados often called

The Bevis Marks Synagogue, London

on the wardens or trustees of Bevis Marks to protect their rights as citizens of the dominions ruled by the British empire. The congregation was also called on from time to time to raise money for the ransom of Jews who had been captured by pirates. (See the preceding chapter.) Now and then they also assisted in transporting rescued Marrano families to safety in Portugal and elswhere.

The congregation at Bevis Marks practiced strict discipline. Punishment for breaking the rules usually meant a fine, or being barred from occupying a seat or taking part in the service. The most extreme penalty was to be denied burial in the cemetery maintained by the congregation. Since Jews as a rule had no opportunity to hold office outside their own religious community, positions of importance in the synagogue were eagerly sought. When an officer was installed he took a solemn oath before the Ark to be diligent, fair and just in the fulfillment of his duties. He was also expected to make a sizable financial contribution to the synagogue.

Some members objected strongly to the strict discipline at Bevis Marks. Prominent among them was a scion of a noted Italian Sephardic family, Isaac Disraeli, whose son Benjamin, born in 1804, would one day become Prime Minister of England. Isaac first startled the congregation by refusing to serve after being elected warden. For this he was fined heavily. He then broke away from the synagogue, abandoning the Jewish faith altogether and baptizing his children.

On the other hand, Bevis Marks could boast that another of its elected wardens, Moses Montefiore (1784–1885) not only remained a loyal benefactor to his own congregation but also became a phenomenal Jewish leader and the most beloved Jewish figure during the nineteenth century for his help to his brethren all over the world and for his contributions to the Holy Land. He was the first English Jew whom Britain honored with a knighthood and he was reputed to be England's leading philanthropist. At Bevis Marks, in the State of Israel and in Jewish history, the memory of Sir Moses and his wife, Lady Judith, live on. Unlike most of the original founders of Bevis Marks, the Montefiore family came to England from Livorno, Italy. In fact, when the synagogue celebrated its bicentenary in 1901, very few descendants of those early leaders were still affiliated with the congregation.*

*Other European synagogues are described and illustrated in Rachel Wischnitzer's definitive work, *The Architecture of the European Synagogue*, Jewish Publication Society, 1964.

Poland: A Refuge through the Centuries

The toleration that permitted Jews to thrive in Protestant countries such as England and Holland did not long prevail in Germany. Indeed, the German reformer, Martin Luther (1483–1546), disappointed that the Jews whom he had befriended had not converted to Protestantism, became a virulent anti-Semite. In the later years of his life, in a campaign to bring about the conversion of the Jews, he began urging Christian princes to destroy synagogues.

All through the sixteenth century, conditions became more and more inhuman for the Jews. In the city of Frankfurt, to cite one example, four thousand Jews were herded into a ghetto, forced to wear badges of identification, and required to pay heavier taxes than any one else. Although they were not formally expelled, it is no wonder that once again many Jews fled Germany in search of a better life.

Ever since the twelfth century, some Jewish refugees had been making their way eastward into Poland. Of all the countries of northern Europe, the Catholic kings and princes of this kingdom had been exceptional in maintaining a consistent policy of friendship toward the Jews. Well-to-do Jews had been welcomed because of their services as bankers and money-lenders. (There are still extant medieval coins that were minted by Jewish officials and carry the names of Polish princes in Hebrew.) In 1264, King Boleslaw, known as "the Pious," issued a charter intended to give Jews complete freedom. In the reign of Casimir the Great, during the fourteenth century, conditions so favored those not often privileged that he was known as "king of the serfs and the Jews." As a result of all this, Jews were able not only to make a living as merchants and craftsmen but, unlike other countries, were also permitted to own land and to work as farmers. Some Jews were trusted with the responsibilities of serving as tax collectors and as managers of royal and baronial estates.

Even during the sixteenth century, when the Counter Reformation (the reactionary movement in Catholic countries which opposed Protestantism) led to new restrictions in many Catholic countries, the Jews continued to find a welcome and to prosper in Catholic Poland. King Sigismund 1 (1506–48) was himself a devout Catholic; but his reign was marked by toleration, and many Jews were given important offices and positions of special honor. Under his successor,

Przedborz: view from the northeast

Interior of Polish wooden synagogue

Sigismund Augustus, the Jews not only flourished but were granted further privileges. In 1551 the king issued a charter that is often called the Magna Charta of Jewish self-government. Its terms formally assured Jews of complete religious freedom and also gave them control of their own schools and even of their own courts of law. In every city and town where Jews lived, they had their own *kahal,* or assembly of elders, who served as governing officials and who cumulatively comprised what amounted almost to a state within a state.

With conditions so favorable, it is not surprising that the Jewish population of Poland grew rapidly. It is estimated that within a century and a half, beginning in 1501, the number of Jews in Poland grew tenfold—from fifty thousand to half a million, which represented about half of European Jewry by the seventeenth century. But unlike their fellow-Jews in England and Holland they settled in small towns scattered throughout the kingdom rather than in large cities.

Polish Synagogues: Folk Art and Fortresses

Hand in hand with this remarkable growth the building of many synagogues grew apace. Those in the larger and more prosperous towns were built of stone or brick. Less imposing, but with a character and charm all their own, were the wooden synagogues that sprang up in the smaller and poorer communities of this forested kingdom. With lumber cheap and more easily handled than stone, synagogues were built by the hundreds. Outwardly they were plain and unpretentious, but their interior decoration was unique. It signified the birth of Jewish folk art of a very special kind.

Talents that might not otherwise have found expression in the arts were given outlet and scope as local artists skillfully carved inscriptions and designs in wood; others painted the walls and ceilings of their houses of worship with scenes from the Bible, with coats of arms and ancient symbols, with the figures of birds and animals that were full of life and movement. The decorations were interwoven with blessings and quotations from the Bible, the prayer book or the sayings of the rabbis. Before the cantor's stand was a decorative Hebrew plaque, the *Shiviti: I have set the Lord always before me* (Psalm 16:8); and the *Omer Table,* counting the 49 days between Passover and the Feast of Weeks. Because it gave them a chance to portray the animal figures they most delighted in, a special favorite of these folk artists was to illustrate the sayings of Judah Ben Tema from The Ethics of the Fathers (5:24): *Be fearless as a leopard, light as an eagle, swift as a deer, and strong as a lion to do the will of your heavenly Father.*

Nearly 100 of these village synagogues were still standing as late as 1939 when the barbaric Nazi invaders swept through Poland burning and destroying everything Jewish. Long before the brutal Nazi catastrophe, life for the Jews of Poland was already far from idyllic. Even under the enlightened rule that gave them such freedom, the nobles quarreled among themselves and with the Church. This made for such unstable conditions that surrounding countries were tempted to try upsetting things still further. For both Russia to the east and Sweden to the north had their greedy eyes on the rich borderlands of Poland. In 1648 Bogdan Chmielnicki led a rebellion of the Cossacks against the Polish landowners as well as the Catholic clergy and the Jews. The massacres then perpetrated on the Jews were as bloody as any they had yet experienced. More than seven hundred Jewish communities were destroyed. The victims, many burned to death with the synagogues, where they had sought shelter, numbered hundreds of thousands. About 1800 synagogue buildings are said to have been destroyed during those tragic years.

The unrest of the times led to an entirely new function for the synagogue. It now became a fortress. During the seventeenth century, therefore, synagogues were built on the outskirts of cities, complete with ramparts and lookout-towers. Permission from the king or the local ruler was needed before such a synagogue could be built; but from the number that were constructed, it is evident that such permission was readily given. It is on record that the fortress-synagogue of Lemberg (now Lvov) was built with the express approval of the city's Catholic bishop. In Lemberg, among other cities, Jewish youths were mobilized for the defense of the synagogue, and anyone able to bear arms who did not appear for military drill was subject to a heavy fine.

Hasidism and the Shtiebel

In the anarchy that followed the Cossack uprising of 1648, the system of Jewish self-government that had flourished for nearly a century broke down. Internal Jewish life was in a state of chaos and under

Fast of Ninth of Av in a Polish synagogue (Painting by Leopold Horowitz)

And at the Wailing Wall in Jerusalem

severe strain. The value of learning, the rabbinic tradition and the role of the rabbi were questioned. In this tragic climate of insecurity and upheaval, a new folk movement took root and blossomed among the Jews of Poland. In some ways it amounted to a social, religious and cultural revolution. The movement was Hasidism, a name derived from the Hebrew word meaning "pious."

The roots of the Hasidic movement can be traced at least as far back as the teachings of the sixteeenth-century mystic Isaac ben Luria, known as "the Ari," whose followers had made their own adaptations of the liturgy and ritual. Those teachings became the main inspiration of another extraordinary and "unworldly" leader, Israel Baal Shem Tov, who was born around the year 1700. He put spiritual religion and purity of the heart above ritual and study, and simple devotion above learning and formal discipline. He taught that all Jews, the ignorant no less than the scholarly, are equal before the Almighty.

This fundamentally new mental as well as emotional attitude is illustrated by two stories, one related to the Baal Shem Tov and the other to a renowned follower. One time, it is told, as the Baal Shem Tov was about to enter the synagogue, he stopped as if he could not get in. *I cannot enter,* he complained, *the place is chock full of learning and prayer from wall to wall and from floor to the ceiling. I cannot push myself in.*

When the people around him were puzzled by his posture and complaint, he added, pointing to the entrance, *The words that pour forth from the worshipers and scholars in there are perfunctory and uttered by rote. They do not come from the heart and are not charged with devotion and true love for the divine. Hence they can not rise to the heaven above but lie heavy as lead on the pews and on the floor and in the aisles. They crowd me out.*

The second tale is attributed to the Rabbi of Kotzk, who once surprised his *hasidim* with this question: *Where does God abide?* Astonished, his devotees replied: *Surely the whole universe is filled with His glory. Nay,* said the Rabbi, *God dwells wherever He is allowed to enter.*

Thus, for the *hasidim* a new spirit permeated worship. The words of the Psalmist, *Serve the Lord with gladness; come before His presence with rejoicing,** were carried out literally and with enthusi-

*Ps. 100:2.

asm. Not only did they express their feelings in congregational chants and singing, but for the first time in fifteen hundred years dancing was brought back into Jewish worship as the *hasidim* linked arms and circled about their *rebbi,* the leader of their congregation. The Hasidic *rebbi* superseded the traditional rabbi, who was learned in the Talmud, as the central figure. Dynasties of *rebiim* (plural of *rebbi*) were established and exist to this day. Hasidism exerted wide appeal and attracted the masses.

This kind of spontaneity and disregard for the established traditional forms naturally met with opposition in many synagogues. Because of this and because the *hasidim* had ideas of their own about what a house of prayer should be, they broke away and set up their own places of worship. The ancient regulation that the synagogue should be the highest building in town was not to their taste. They believed the opposite. Usually they constituted a small intimate group and were quite satisfied with a small building. Modest and unassuming, the *hasidim* delighted in calling the synagogue a *shtiebel*—a Yiddish word meaning "little house." For they were mainly poor people who found joy in living, no matter how underprivileged and deprived they were. The *shtiebel* echoed to their lilting songs as they worshiped. But more than that, it became a truly communal gathering place where they shared meals, or sat about the table learning the holy books, chanting Psalms, listening to their *rebbi* speak, or to their colleagues telling stories about the *rebbi.* It was the *hasidim* who invested with ecstatic celebration the traditional *Shalosh Seudot,* the "third" or afternoon meal on the Sabbath, and the *Melavah Malkah,* the farewell party for Queen Sabbath after the holy day of rest came to an end.

Every *rebbi* had a style of his own, which was adopted by his followers. Some swayed back and forth, some from side to side as they prayed. Some prayed aloud at the top of their voices as they paced around in the *shtiebel.* Others were silent, turning inward while they prayed. Many chanted from the Book of Psalms. At prayer and study, the *hasidim* of the early days in Poland wore a *gartel* (woven belt or girdle) about their waists to symbolize their concentration on matters which concern the upper part of the body, the head and the heart, as distinct from the more worldly concerns symbolized by their lower parts. Many wore a black or brown *caftan* reaching to the knee or the ankle, and a round, brimmed fur-trimmed hat known as a *shtreimel*— a costume seen among the *hasidim* of New York, Israel and elsewhere even to day. For it was inevitable that this movement that had its beginning among the Jews of Poland and Eastern Europe should find its way in time to the Jewish communities of Europe, Israel and the New World.

The influence of Hasidism continues to be felt in literature, drama, music, and the visual arts. Through books by Martin Buber, Isaac Leib Peretz, Isaac B. Singer and others, and by means of plays like *The Dybbuk*, by S. Ansky, as well as music and dance recordings, Hasidism has made a rich contribution to Jewish life which is deeply felt to this very day. In Israel, colonies and institutions have been established by Hasidic dynasties such as those of Lubavitch (which has a world-wide network of schools and organizations), Bobov, Tzanz and others. Despite the current prevailing mood of skepticism and alienation from Jewish life, the Hasidic movement, because of its simplicity, semi-mystical piety and "folksy" ways of life, is still— though reduced in numbers—widespread, vital and promising.

Bais Hamedrosh

Closely resembling the *shtiebel* in its unpretentiousness, modesty and "folksiness" was the *Bais Hamedrosh*. It was not necessarily Hasidic in content, but like the *shtiebel* it was a place of religious spontaneity and of freedom from so-called decorum. The *daveners* (worshipers) knew the prayer book and participated in the service not under the direction of a rabbi or *hazzan*, but responding, setting their own pace, singing, chanting, accompanying the prayer-leader as the spirit moved them. It was a wholehearted, whole-bodied involvement. The *daveners* had a feeling of togetherness because they believed that a "yid" must *daven* without any special devices or contrivances to involve him.

Above all, the *Bais Hamedrosh* was a place of study. Jews met in various groups, depending on their level of learning, to *leren* (learn). For the plain folk there was a *Hevrah Tehillim*— the group for recitation of Psalms, usually in a unique plaintive chant. For the more scholarly there was a *Hevrah Ein Yaakov* (Fountain of Jacob) — a group concentrating on a work comprising a popular compilation of legends in Hebrew drawn from the Talmud.

More prestigious groups were the *Hevrah Mishnayot*—the students of Mishnah, the legal code in Hebrew which forms the basis of the Talmud; and for the scholars, *a Hevrah Shas* [Talmud]. And scattered in the room were individual students of the Talmud who studied independently on their own. Study followed *davening* and was as informal and as hearty. Everyone was welcome; some participated and others just listened. To this day this robust aspect of synagogue life still exists in many synagogues. In one of his stirring poems Hayim Nahman Bialik, the poet laureate of the Jewish people, rightfully called the *Bais Hamedrosh* the Source of Strength, the fountainhead that has shaped the "soul of the people."

We cite here the *Bais Hamedrosh* as drawn by Sholom Asch in vignette form in his book *Salvation*:

> It was still early in the evening and in the Tehillim [Psalms] Room blind Reb Leibush was sitting at the so-called *Hand-workers* table, going through the legends of the Talmud with the workmen. Quite at the back, near the washing basins, some ten men were sitting on low benches: furriers, hatters, tailors and cobblers, who practiced their trades only in winter, and in summer cultivated vegetables or fruit. Their faces were furrowed by rain and snow, their hair disheveled, their beards unkempt, their bodies bent by the winds. They sat with simple, credulous faces at the table and gazed dumbly at the torn, thumbed books that lay before them. At the head of the table, where blind Reb Leibush sat, a dripping wax candle burned in a cast-iron candlestick; it was, of course, superfluous, for the blind man knew his lesson by heart.
>
> Reb Leibush was a strange character, such as is only to be found in the by-gone Jewish communities shut off from the rest of the world. He was in a manner of speaking the "Rabbi" of the Psalm Fellowship which the small hand-workers and market vendors of the town had formed. Every Friday and before every feast day they sent to the *Tempelgasse*, where he lived, a few coins wrapped in paper. For the most part, his payment was in kind and consisted of food. Every Friday the fisherman Melech gave the blind man's wife a small fish for the Sabbath, and Selig the butcher often flung into her lap a bone to which a little fat still clung. When necessary the cobblers of the place finished at their own expense a pair of boots for the blind man or his wife.

In return Reb Leibush translated for the hand-workers the Psalms and other parts of the Holy Scripture.

And the feelings of one of the plain people are captured in the following description of Yechiel, the hero of the same novel:

> On such a day, which Yechiel dedicated to God, the bare Tehillim Room [shtiebel] with its poorly clad workmen looked quite different. A boundless joy filled him at the thought that he too was one of the children of Israel and was permitted to live in their midst. Abraham was his forefather. He, Yechiel, had also stood on Sinai. The little Psalm Room was God's dwelling. On such days he asked no favor from God. He prayed only in honor of God, and the words of the prayers took on deeper meaning —he could read into them whatever he liked. Suddenly they revealed themselves to him, and a casket locked until now stood open before him. Yechiel gave the words his own meaning; he had the power to fill them with content and substance.
>
> And while he stood in the faint dawn beside the poor people, whose cries for help and desperate petitions beat against the cold walls of the low-walled room, he was in a different world. The room with its four walls and its roof vanished and Yechiel hovered in a sea of clouds. God was no longer an abstract conception to him but a living being in whose presence he stood and with whom he spoke. He asked nothing of Him, but only rejoiced in Him. He was happy to be allowed to come so near God and to tell Him how greatly he rejoiced in Him, how ardently he loved Him.
>
> This sense was with him not only during the hour of prayer, but afterwards as well. When he returned from his prayers he did not hastily wash and sit down to breakfast as usual, that he might set off for the village at once. On such days he told himself, "Now I am going home to eat to your glory, God." With this thought he sat down at the wretched table. He washed, recited the blessing, dipped his slice of bread in salt and began slowly and devoutly to eat. While he did so he pictured to himself that God was sitting opposite him, seeing that he was eating in His honor.*

*Sholom Asch *Salvation*, New York, Putnam, 1934, pp. 48, 62f.

When, in the latter part of the nineteenth and at the beginning of the twentieth centuries, the hamlets and towns of the Russian "pale" were emptied of Jews as they emigrated to the unbounded, longed-for shores of America, it was the *Bais Hamedrosh* which they promptly transplanted in the ghettos of New York and other cities of the Atlantic seaboard. It sustained them spiritually until they were able to erect the synagogue edifices which are described in the later chapters.

Day of Atonement in Synagogue

XI

The Synagogue in the New World

When One Rises Another Falls

Solomon Schechter, who was mentioned in Chapter VIII, in connection with the Cairo *Genizah*, made a noteworthy comment about the New World, to which he came in 1901. It reads:

> On the day on which King Solomon married the daughter of Pharaoh, the Rabbis narrate, there came down the angel Gabriel. He put a reed in the sea, which, by means of the slime that adhered to it, formed itself. . . . into a large island, on which the City of Rome was built—an event with which the troubles of Israel began. If our poets had had some of the imaginative powers of the Rabbis, they would have perceived in Columbus another angel, and in the discovery of America, not the triumph of Spain, but the punishment of Spain. For it was America which was destined. . . , to give a death blow to all the principles for which Spain stood. Persecution and fanaticism were the things which Spain wished to enforce. Liberty of conscience and tolerance were the doctrines which America gave the world. These two contrasts could not exist on the side of one another. As the Rabbis say of Jacob and Esau, God's world, large as it is, is too small to keep both; when the one rises, the other falls.*

*Norman Bentwich, *Solomon Schechter*, East and West Library, London, 1947.

125

The first Jewish settlers to arrive in the New World were Marranos who came to try their fortunes in the Portuguese and Spanish colonies of Mexico, the West Indies and South America. By the middle of the seventeenth century, some were already prospering as traders or as owners of sugar plantations. In 1631 the Dutch managed to seize control of the Portuguese colony that is now Brazil. As a result, the number of Marranos there increased, especially in the city of Recife (Pernambuco) and some of them renounced their assumed faith and began worshiping openly as Jews. When the Portuguese reconquered Brazil in 1654, these Marranos were no longer safe. Fearing the long arm of the dreaded Inquisition would stretch across the Atlantic Ocean to seize them, they again fled for their lives.

Jews Settle in Curaçao

Many of those who fled made their way to islands in the Caribbean. One group founded a colony in Surinam (Dutch Guiana) which still exists. A larger group founded a colony in 1654 on the island of Curaçao, just off the coast of South America. Among the historic sights of Willemstad, the island's capital, is the cemetery they consecrated in 1659. Its crowded stones contain hundreds of fascinating inscriptions in Spanish, Portuguese and Hebrew. Not far from the cemetery is the synagogue of the Congregation Mikveh Israel (Hope of Israel). Erected in 1732, it is the oldest such building in the Western Hemisphere still in active use. And unlike Bevis Marks and various Sephardic synagogues throughout the world, many of the families who worship there to this day have belonged to the congregation as families for two and even three centuries.

The Curaçao synagogue covers almost an entire city block in the main business district of Willemstad, a section that during the seventeenth century was the center of the Jewish colony. (Indeed in Europe and the Americas early synagogue buildings are situated on what are to-day choice locations.) The close ties of the community with the Portuguese synagogue in Amsterdam are still evident. The four brass candelabra suspended from the ceiling and the eight huge brass candlesticks on the reader's platform are exact replicas of those in Amsterdam, and are older than the building itself. All the woodwork is mahogany, including the reader's desk, which stands at the center of the hall, and the richly carved Ark, which is fifteen feet wide and seventeen feet high. Riveted to two mahogany tablets at

Curaçao Synagogue interior

Curaçao Synagogue exterior

the top of the Ark are silver plaques inscribed with the Ten Commandments. In the corner is the special chair on which the circumcision of infant boys was performed long ago. The wooden floor of the synagogue is kept covered with sand. Whether this custom began as a symbolic reminder of the wanderings of the Israelites through the desert, or simply as a means to muffle the sound of heavy boots, is no longer certain.

Beginnings in North America: Shearith Israel

Another band of refugees from Recife, Brazil, ventured farther north, to the Dutch colony of New Amsterdam, later to become New York. They numbered twenty-three when they arrived in 1654 with little more than the clothes they were wearing. They had difficulties with the Dutch, and these did not end when the British conquered New Amsterdam in 1664. But in the interim, despite restrictions and troubles, they struck roots and established a congregation that has continued to thrive from that day to this.

Their first regular house of worship was on what is now South William Street, then known as Mill Street. A gristmill had been built there soon after the Dutch settlers arrived, and in it the members of a Dutch Reformed Church had held their first services in 1628. When the Dutch built a church of their own, the Congregration Shearith Israel (Remnant of Israel) began holding services in the mill. (It was characteristic of the newcomers that they did not hesitate to buy vacated church buildings, a practice unheard of in the old country.) They continued to worship in the mill until about 1675, when they rented a frame house which had been a residence a few doors away from the mill and remodeled it into a synagogue. In 1728 the congregation bought a plot of land adjoining, and in 1730 with the substantial financial help from synagogues in Boston,Barbados, Curaçao and Surinam, the first synagogue built on North American soil was dedicated.

Like some synagogues in Europe, this one was built inside a courtyard with its entrance facing away from the street. Beside it were several buildings which the congregation also owned. One of them was used as a ritual bath, while others were occupied at various times by the cantor, the ritual slaughterer and the sexton. It was here that the poor, the sick and the wayfarers were cared for. As in olden times, this too was a complex of structures serving the religious and communal needs of Jews. And as was customary in synagogues of the time, the women's gallery had a separate entrance, opposite that used by the men.

Since the Sephardic Jews who constituted that early congregation were nearly all Marranos, they were referred to in the early records of the city as the "Portuguese nation." Some had lived so long as secret Jews, we are told, that they—especially some of the women—found it difficult to break themselves of the habit of saying Hebrew prayers while fingering a Catholic rosary, or even of crossing themselves when they heard the town clock strike.

During the turbulent years while the struggle between the colonists and the British was escalating, most of the members sided with the colonists. Perhaps the most outspoken of the patriots was Gershom Mendez Seixas (1745–1816), who served for many years as rabbi. In August 1776, when British ships commanded by Lord Howe appeared in New York Harbor, Seixas closed the synagogue and fled taking with him the Torah scrolls owned by the congregation. The building was reopened for services by three other Jews who supported the British, and who prevailed on them not to requisition it for the use of their troops, as had happened to most of the public buildings of the city. Nevertheless, the building was not entirely spared; during the Revolution, soldiers broke in and damaged some of the furnishings.

The war over, Seixas and other members who had fled returned to the city, and in 1818 the synagogue was rebuilt. In 1833 the congregation moved to Crosby Street on what is now called New York's Lower East Side, where gas lamps replaced candlelight. In 1860, following the northward movement of the people, it moved still further uptown, to Nineteenth Street and Fifth Avenue; and still later took up its present location at Seventieth Street and Central Park West. In the cornerstone which was laid on May 20, 1896, was deposited among other articles a package of earth from the Holy Land brought by the uncle of the congregation's president, Commodore Uriah P. Levy.* Here, in 1954, the three hundredth anniversary of the original Jewish settlement in North America was celebrated. During the ceremony, two of the Torah scrolls that Seixas had taken with him on his flight were carried into the synagogue by a

*Uriah Phillips Levy (1792–1862) was flag officer of the Mediterranean Squadron, then the highest post in the U.S. Navy.

procession of Jewish leaders. A proclamation was read ". . . . *to offer thanks unto the Lord for all the blessings bestowed on us in America . . . and to rededicate ourselves to the ideals of our faith within the freedom of American democracy.*"

The Touro Synagogue: A National Monument

The Rhode Island colony founded by Roger Williams practiced greater religious toleration than any other in the New World. It is therefore not surprising that synagogues should have been founded there. The first of these, dating to 1658, was Congregation Jeshuat Israel (Salvation of Israel), in Newport, composed of a group of Sephardic Jews from Spain, Portugal, Holland, and the West Indies. More than a century elapsed before a synagogue was finally built. Named for its first rabbi, Isaac Touro, Jeshuat Israel was dedicated in December on the first day of Hanukkah 1763—a date commemorative of a similar re-dedication which the Maccabeans had celebrated nearly two thousand years previously (165 B.C.E.) in the Temple they had restored.

The building, designed by the colonial architect Peter Harrison, who also designed the King's Chapel in Boston, is a beautiful blend of the American colonial style with the style of the Portuguese synagogue in Amsterdam and the Bevis Marks in London. Measuring thirty-five by forty-five feet, it stands at an angle, so that the wall containing the Holy Ark faces directly east. Three treasured Torah scrolls, inscribed on vellum, have been continuously kept in a wooden cupboard on that wall; one was already two centuries old when it was brought to Newport from Amsterdam.

Overhead is a domed ceiling, painted light blue with a sprinkling of silver stars. On the north wall is a raised seat for the elders, and a little to the west of the center is the raised *bimah*, or pulpit, for the reading of the Torah. Next to the reading desk is a small stairway that leads to a secret passage underneath the building. The exit from this underground tunnel has long been closed, and its original purpose is no longer known. Running along three sides of the hall, and supported by twelve columns symbolizing the twelve tribes of Israel, is the women's gallery. It is entered by an outer stairway which leads into a separate building that was used as a school, and which also contains an oven in which unleavened bread was baked for Passover.

Touro Synagogue, Providence, Rhode Island

An ancient matzah board used in preparing the flat bread may still be seen there today.

From 1781 to 1784, this historic synagogue served as the meeting place of the Rhode Island General Assembly. For a time, the State Supreme Court also met within its walls, and in 1790 George Washington was greeted there by the congregation. The building's intimate association with the early days of the Republic led to its designation in 1946 as a national historic site—the first Jewish shrine in the United States to be thus honored.

Early Congregations in Philadelphia and the South

The third oldest Jewish congregation in North America, Mikveh Israel (Hope of Israel) was established in Philadelphia around the beginning of the eighteenth century. The solemn and ceremonious consecration of the synagogue on a Sabbath day in 1782 was led by a Polish Jew, Hayim Salomon, who later helped to finance the newly founded republic. Benjamin Franklin was a contributor, as were other Christian friends. Today Mikveh Israel is located near the center of Philadelphia; plans are under way to move it to a site near Independence Hall in the newly reconstructed historic Society Hill section of Philadelphia.

Other groups of Jewish settlers were less successful in establishing a congregation. In Georgia, for example, Jewish settlers arrived as early as 1733, soon after General Oglethorpe, the founder of the colony. There were forty in the group, and they brought with them a Torah scroll. A second scroll, as well as a Hanukkah candelabrum, Hebrew prayer books, and other equipment arrived with a second group of forty or fifty who came later that same year. They held services and acquired a little plot of ground for a cemetery. In 1770, nearly forty years later, a group of six Jewish families were still worshiping in a room that the revolutionary patriot Mordecai Sheftall had furnished as a chapel in his own house in Savannah. It was not until 1790 that a congregation was finally established, and it had no building until 1820.

In Charleston, South Carolina, the fourth oldest congregation in North America, Beth Elohim Unveh Shalom (House of God and Mansion of Peace), was founded during the High Holy Days in the fall of 1749. In 1775 its cantor, Isaac da Costa, traveled to New York to ask the members of Congregation Shearith Israel for help in build-

ing a synagogue. But with times already hard and the revolution
brewing, his request was refused. The noted historian of early American Jewry, Jacob Rader Marcus, tells us that *Charleston's struggle to
have a house of worship was typical of almost every American Jewish
community of the period.* In the years between 1749 and 1794 the
worshipers of Beth Elohim moved from one place to another, four
in all, before they built a synagogue. The fourth building was a remodeled cotton-gin manufactory and was called the "Old Synagogue." By the 1780's a well-rounded community organization existed in the city. In 1794 the "New Synagogue," then the largest and
most impressive in the Western Hemisphere, was built.*

Leadership of the Synagogue

In some ways, the synagogue was even more important to the Jewish
communities of the early years in America than it had been in
Europe. It was literally the only community organization, and the
lives of its members were centered on it in a way that is not easy for
us to imagine. It appeared to them vital to adhere to the old rigid life
style until they adjusted to the New World; otherwise they feared
they might disintegrate. A taste of the atmosphere that prevailed is
communicated in the account set down by Naphtali Taylor Philips,
scion of an old New York family, concerning the early days of
Shearith Israel in New York:

> In respect of family life in the congregation before the Revolu-
> tion, the board of trustees had considerable power in the ad-
> ministration of the lives of men. They exercised a good deal of
> power. . . , very much in the same manner which the Portuguese
> congregation in Amsterdam, Holland, had done in its day. And,
> of course, our congregration took all its inspirations largely from
> the Amsterdam congregration . . . and in Amsterdam the author-
> ity of the *mahamad* was supreme. The *mahamad,* the trustees,
> as we call them now, were the absolute masters of the life and
> liberty and fortunes. In New York they very much endeavored
> to perpetuate that idea, but it did not always work. Always there
> was a great deal of friction in regard to those matters. It was

Early American Jewry, Volume II, Philadelphia, Jewish Publication Society of America, 1953.

never accepted. . . . There never was a time, whether it was the spirit of the new country or not, when there was that implicit obedience from the congregation to these edicts that there had been in Amsterdam. The *mahamad* exercised their power; they declared a person outside the law if he did this, that, or the other thing. He could not be married and all that sort of thing if he did not change the manner of keeping his house kosher, and so on, but in the last analysis, these things were rarely enforced. Sometimes when they were enforced, it was only after a great battle, and they would even go to the courts . . .*

In Chapter V the function of the *Ma-amadot* was described. In the worship of ancient Israel—as we have previously noted—these were the representatives of the people who stood by while the sacrifice was offered in the Temple at Jerusalem. We also pointed out that scholars regard the *Ma-amadot* as the real origin of the synagogue. Thus, in both name and position, the *mahamad* are, in a sense, the direct descendants of the Palestinian *Ma-amadot*.

The next chapter will trace the history of the various functionaries of the synagogue—the rabbi, the cantor, the sexton and others. But it is worth noting here that in colonial North America the rabbi did not have the prestige he had enjoyed in Europe. This was partly because those early congregations could not afford to pay a salary to a full-time rabbi; at the beginning, in fact, even the cantor, who generally took the more active part in the service, was a volunteer. Another reason for the rabbi's lack of prominence was that very few of those early settlers were scholars, and none had been trained as rabbis or ordained as such.

Therefore, until the nineteenth century the lay officials were the real leaders in the synagogues of North America. They were elected more or less democratically by the congregation, and as in European synagogues, were generally men of prominence and often of wealth. The chief presiding officer in the Sephardic synagogues of the time was the *parnas*. The word means "provider," but it has also come to be synonymous, in some cases, with "autocrat." Another of Mr. Philips's family recollections of the early days of Shearith Israel in New York suggests the reason for this:

*This and the quotations that follow are from Naphtali Taylor Philips, American Jewish Archives, June, 1954, in an article entitled "Unwritten History."

Mr. Luis Moses Gomez was president at the time the synagogue was consecrated in 1730, and during the time of his presidency and for many years afterwards, when the Gomezes were present in the synagogue, the lady, the wife of the *parnas*, had a separate seat in the gallery for herself, a sort of lady's *banca*. The seat which the parnas sits on is called *banca*, the Spanish word for bench, and the wife had the *banca* upstairs in the gallery the same way.... Then quite a controversy arose because, when one of the Gomezes ceased to be parnas, the (erstwhile) lady parnas wanted to sit on the *banca* anyhow.... They did not take it away for many years afterward; it remained there, but she did not occupy it.

Secessions and Growth

For nearly a century Shearith Israel dominated the religious and social lives of the Jews. The ritual, liturgy and pronunciation was Sephardic. But as the immigration grew its dominance began to be threatened. In April 1825 the rift came. A Mr. Cohen, who was called to the Torah refused to donate the two shillings for charity which was obligatory. He was made to appear before the *mahamad* where he was charged with disobedience. Mr. Cohen claimed ignorance, discrimination, and financial hardship. And although the defendant was excused and the *mahamad* even went so far as to offer to rescind the two-shilling offering, he was not appeased.

The Ashkenazic dissidents petitioned to hold their own services, a more equitable distribution of the synagogue honors and a reduction in the amount of the offering. They were also critical of the laxity in observance and piety and planned to be more strict among its group. They assured the congregation, however, that they would not break away.

The division became sharp. Shearit Israel decided that future members would be permitted to join the synagogue by vote only. When in September 1825 only two of sixteen applicants were accepted, the Ashkenazim seceded. Thus was born the first Ashkenazic congregation Bnai Jeshurun.

As the Jewish community grew further splintering went on apace. Most of the newcomers came from the Ashkenazic regions in Europe. Ten years later was organized Congregation Shaare Zedek.

Thus by 1860 there were some twenty-five congregations which drew their membership from people who sought to replicate the synagogue of their old hometowns. At first these synagogues were located on the Lower East Side but gradually as their congregants moved uptown the synagogues followed them. What happened in New York occurred in other large Jewish communities on the continent.*

As at Bevis Marks in London, the usual way of maintaining order and decorum in the congregation among early North American synagogues was by imposing a fine. The noted Jewish historian Prof. Salo W. Baron writes that in 1810 the young congregation Rodeph Shalom of Philadelphia fined its members 25 cents for absences that were inexcusable or for leaving the house of worship before the prayers were concluded.† In Savannah, some of the congregation of Mikveh Israel were plantation owners, who did not always dress in a manner the leadership considered proper; so in order to maintain decorum, a rule was passed that no one could be called up for the reading of the Torah if he was wearing boots. Since it was one of the responsibilities of the *parnas* to choose those to be honored in this way, he was in a position to enforce the ruling. It was also his responsibility to ask for contributions and to keep the records of the congregation.

In 1848 the German Jewish immigration began. Small *(minyan)* synagogues began to spring up in various parts of the country even in the far west. The new comers brought with them the ways of life from the old home. They even imported rabbis who delivered their sermons in German. The chief lay leader was now known as *gabbai*, meaning collector of dues and charitable contributions.

By 1776 there were probably no more than 2500 Jews. By 1880 the number had grown a hundred fold. When in 1881–1882 pogroms broke out in Russia there began huge waves of immigration. By 1914 some two million Jews came to the New World changing radically the complexion of the Jewish community and synagogue life. These significant transformations will be described in the chapters that follow.

*Grinstein, Hyman R. *The Rise of the Jewish Community of New York (1654–1860)*, Jewish Publication Society, 1945, Chap. 3.
†*The Jewish Community*, Volume II, p 131.

XII
The Officiants of the Synagogue

The Rabbi

As noted in the preceding chapter, the part played by the rabbi in colonial America was relatively unimportant. To one familiar with the North American synagogue of today—in which the rabbi has a full-time position, is paid a respectable salary, and is recognized as the religious and spiritual leader of the congregation—this comes as a surprise.

That does not mean, of course, that the position of rabbi is new. On the contrary, not only is it at least as old as the synagogue itself, but the two cannot really be separated at any time in their history. The word "rabbi" comes from *rav*, meaning "great" or "distinguished" and the connotation is "master" or "teacher." From early times it was a title of distinction earned by men of learning who were recognized interpreters of the Law. The title as we understand it today is first mentioned in the twelfth century. In various ways, at least to some extent, rabbis were supported by the community. The origin of this practice may be that the heads of the Babylonian academies, because they were the leading scholars of their day, were actually paid salaries. But in general the sages, whose thought constitutes the Talmud, no matter how learned and famous they eventually became, continued to support themselves. Most often they labored as merchants, artisans, or even shoemakers and blacksmiths. For teaching was deemed a religious service and according to tradition was dispensed without payment of fees. (Compare with the statement in Ethics of the Fathers 4:5.)

This was also true of the great scholars of medieval Europe. Rashi kept a vineyard; Maimonides was a physician; Abrabanel was a financier. Even in their time, however, as commerce developed and money came into wider use as a means of exchange, it was becoming customary to pay a rabbi for his services. By the fourteenth century the practice was already being taken more or less for granted. Even so, the duties a rabbi was expected to perform were quite different from those of today. His authority as spiritual leader was never questioned. Above all, he was a teacher and a guide on Jewish Law. He served as judges do today in courts of law. He also officiated at marriages and burials; for these services he was paid a fee. In addition, he had charge of the arrangements that were necessary for keeping households and communal undertakings ritually proper. In the synagogue itself, however, he had little more to do than preach on questions of *Halakhah* (Law) two or three times a year, usually on the Sabbaths before Yom Kippur and Passover. The rabbi was shown great respect. For example, after the service he left first while the congregants waited. The kind of administrative work that nowadays makes being a rabbi a full-time job fell, as we have seen, to the president of the congregation and to the *shamash* (see below).

In the days of the Talmudic academies in Europe and elsewhere, a scholar earned the title of rabbi only after completing an intensive course of study in the Scriptures, Talmud and Codes of Law. In very early times, once he had been so recognized, he was received into the brotherhood of scholars in a solemn ceremony known as the *semikha*—a Hebrew word referring to the laying on of hands, which was a part of the ritual. The tradition of the *semikha* is based on the answer to the plea voiced by Moses. When he knew that he himself was not to enter the Promised Land, he said: *Let the Lord. . . . appoint a man permitted to lead the people into Canaan, who shall lead them. . . . that the congregation of the Lord shall not be as sheep which have no shepherd.* According to the account in Numbers 27:12–23, *The Lord* said, *'Take Joshua the son of Nun, a man in whom is the spirit, and lay your hand upon him. . . . and you shall commission him in their sight. . . . You shall invest him with some of your authority that all the congregation of Israel may obey.* The "laying on of hands" was, as early as Talmudic times, communicated orally by leading rabbis and later by a written document.

In medieval times, to qualify as a rabbi it was necessary to have a document from another rabbi—preferably one who had attained fame and a high reputation—investing the holder of the document with rabbinic authority and declaring that he was known to be a devout man, of good character, and equipped with the learning necessary to hand down decision in matters of Jewish Law. This document was referred to and became known as *semikha*.

The ceremony of ordination by the laying on of hands has continued in simplified form down to the present, and is usually conferred on rabbinical students when they have finished their course at a rabbinic seminary. Among those receiving the *semikha*, some are singled out as qualified by their studies in the Talmud and *Halakhah* to decide on questions involving matters of law and ritual, and to grant divorces in keeping with religious laws. Not all graduates of Jewish seminaries receive such *semikha*, but all who are ordained are invested with the authority to preach, to teach, and to officiate at marriages and burials and the like. This authority to perform marriages is recognized by the state in which the rabbi resides and functions.

Generally speaking in Europe and in Israel, the rabbi is still regarded mainly as a teacher and as a man devoted to studying the Scriptures, the Talmud, the Commentaries and Codes. In the United States, his work as a community leader tends to take priority. But here as there, he is above all the man charged with transmitting the heritage of his people to the succeeding generations.

The Sheliah Tzibur (Prayer Leader), Hazzan, or Cantor

We noted in Chapter XI how Isaac da Costa, the leader of Congregation Beth Elohim in Charleston, also led the service. In this capacity he served voluntarily. There were no paid officials in the synagogues of colonial North America. In those days, greater importance was attached to the position of the cantor, or *hazzan*, than to any other functionary of the synagogue. Jacob Marcus writes that *it was the duty of the hazzan to chant the services, and to be present and to officiate at weddings and funerals, circumcisions, and similar religious affairs. Above all he had to answer to the* parnas. *He rarely preached, and then only by request. Frequently he taught the young.**

*Ibid.

The position of the *hazzan* like that of rabbi, is quite ancient. No one is certain what the title meant originally. It may have been derived from the Assyrian word *hazanu* meaning "overseer," or from the Hebrew word *hozeh* meaning "seer." There is, however, no doubt that the duties themselves go back to the days of the Temple in Jerusalem, where the *hazzan* was in charge of the vessels used during the sacrifice and where he acted as assistant to the priests. When the synagogue came into being, it became the responsibility of the *hazzan* to take care of the Torah scroll, to keep the lamps trimmed and lighted, and to announce the approach of the Sabbath and holy days from the roof of the synagogue or in the streets of the Jewish quarter. Thus, in the early days, the *hazzan's* duties were more or less the same as those that are now assigned to the *shamash*, or sexton.

We read in the Talmud that during the time when a synagogue stood in the precincts of the Temple, it was the ceremonial custom, on Yom Kippur (Day of Atonement), for the *hazzan* to open the scroll of the Law to the proper place, and then carry it to the *Rosh Knesset,* the highest lay officer of the congregation. He in his turn would deliver it to the Deputy High Priest to read to the worshipers. On the *Sukkot* festival during a sabbatical year, the sequence would be carried one step further as the High Priest delivered the scroll to be read by the King himself.

The changes that transformed the duties of the *hazzan* of ancient times into those of the cantor of today came about gradually. In the synagogue of Alexandria (Egypt) the hall was so large that it was impossible to hear every word as the Scripture was being read. Consequently, it was customary for the *hazzan* to hold up a special piece of cloth as a signal for the congregation to respond with "Amen" or "Hallelujah." In the early Middle Ages *hazzanim* were also known to improvise prayers. To guard against errors and mistakes in the chanting of the liturgy, prompters or "supporters" were appointed to stand by to oversee and prompt the prayer leader when necessary. These "helpers" eventually became the synagogue choir as we know it today.

An appealing mental image of the *hazzan* is evoked by the fervor and humility of a prayer of petition composed by an anonymous *hazzan* of the Middle Ages. Indeed, it was so stirring that it was included as the opening meditation with which, in our time, the *hazzan* introduces the *Mussaf,* i.e., the Additional Service for Rosh Hashanah and Yom Kippur. The opening is as follows:

> In deep fear and humility I stand before You, God on High. I have come to plead before You on behalf of Your people. Hear my supplication. . . . Though unworthy of my sacred task. . . . though imperfect, I bow before Your Presence and ask compassion for those who asked me to plead for them. . . . Accept my prayers. . . . Do not blame the people for my sins. Put them not to shame because of my faults. . . . Accept my prayer as though I were well qualified. . . . May our shortcomings be pardoned by your love for love makes up for all sins. . . . And let my prayer pour out without stumbling. . . .

Further on in the same service we read of the feelings of the people in the congregation toward their *hazzan:*

> Inspire the lips of those who stand before You. Teach them what to say; instruct them how to speak; grant them what they ask and show them the way to glorify You. . . . They lead Your people to seek You. . . . The eyes of Your people are upon their leaders and the eyes of the leaders are toward You. Do not let them falter with their tongue nor err in their speech that the many who put their trust in them be not put to shame.

All Jews participated in the synagogue service. It was therefore perfectly natural for the worshipers to join in the responses and later in the *piyutim,* the chanted liturgy which developed during the Middle Ages. As the liturgy became more and more elaborate, increasing care had to be exercised to make sure that it was correctly chanted or sung. Thus it was that around the fourteenth century the special office of cantor came into being.

To understand how that office developed, it is necessary to recall the changes that had been taking place in Jewish life throughout Europe. One of these was a decline in the knowledge of Hebrew. In southern Europe, Ladino, a mixture of Spanish and Hebrew, evolved as the spoken language of Sephardic Jews. Among the Ashkenazim to the north and east, the everyday language was Yiddish, a mixture of German and Hebrew. In Moslem countries the vernacular was

Arabic and Hebrew, and so on. This meant that for ordinary people, even those who received an education, Hebrew became increasingly difficult to read. As a result, it happened not infrequently that a man called up for the reading of the Torah might be unable to chant the portion assigned him. And as the festival *piyyutim* became more and more complex, only a trained musician with a good voice as well as a knowledge of the Hebrew words could be expected to perform them properly.

Thus it was that the *hazzan*, devoting himself more and more to that aspect of the synagogue service, came to be looked upon first of all as a singer and musician. The importance of tradition and the prestige of the office is still strong. This explains a resolution passed by the Cantors' Assembly of the United Synagogue of America, asking that members of their body be accorded the title of *hazzan*, as the spiritual leader of the congregation is called rabbi. Today, in many synagogues this title rather than "cantor" is indeed applied.

In the latter part of the nineteenth century, with the large immigration of Russian and Polish Jews who established synagogues using the Ashkenazic ritual, the role of the cantor grew in importance. Cantors of great prestige, such as "Yosele" (Joseph) Rosenblatt, Zavel Kwartin and Mordecai Hershman, attracted large congregations of worshipers. In fact, people flocked to the synagogues more for their singing than for the rabbis' sermons. They were usually accompanied by all-male choirs.

Cantors performed at vocal concerts where they were the star performers, drawing large numbers of people who paid comparatively high prices for admission. They also made phonograph records of liturgical music which sold extremely well; indeed cantorial records are still very popular. Cantors like Richard Tucker and Jan Peerce have also achieved renown as opera singers.

The leading rabbinical seminaries—Hebrew Union College–Jewish Institute of Religion, Jewish Theological Seminary and Yeshiva University—conduct departments for the training of cantors on the same high levels as for the training of rabbis and religious school teachers.

The Darshan or Interpreter

For reasons not unrelated to the growth of the office of cantor, another synagogue official came into being who has since then largely

Priestly blessing from a medieval illuminated Machsor

Medieval synagogue scene, woodcut, 1530

disappeared. This was the *darshan*. The term comes from the Hebrew word meaning to seek, i.e., to delve into the meaning of the text, hence—an interpreter. His duties may be traced to ancient times, when Aramaic was the spoken tongue throughout much of the Middle East. Among the Jews, even those of Babylonia and elsewhere in the Middle East, Hebrew had not been forgotten. It was the tongue of the motherland, the language of the Holy Scriptures, and the common bond uniting all who learned to read. Although their day-to-day business was carried on in Aramaic, Hebrew remained for them the language of their religion and culture.

As Hebrew ceased to be spoken, the rabbis became concerned about teaching the Torah in such a way that it would be understood by everyone. In Alexandria, during the second century B.C.E., Greek-speaking Jews took matters into their own hands and translated the entire Bible into Greek. This translation, as indicated earlier, was known as the Septuagint (from the Latin word for "seventy" —a reference to the legend that it was the work of seventy scholars), and for several reasons the rabbis of Babylonia and Palestine were troubled by it. For one thing, it contained variations from the accepted Hebrew text. For another, they feared that because of its great popularity, it would lead to a break with the Hebrew tradition and language (as it indeed did). At the same time, they recognized that the problem which had led to the translation of the Septuagint was no less real in the regions where Aramaic was the spoken language. This led to a translation of the Scriptures into Aramaic; it was known as the Targum.

At first the Targum was transmitted orally. And as a means of preventing errors of the kind that had crept into the Septuagint, the rabbis introduced an interpreter *(meturgeman)* into the synagogue service. (From this word is derived the English term "dragoman," a travelers' guide who acts as translator.) Following the reading of each verse of the Torah, and after every third verse in the Haftarah, or prophetic portion, it was the duty of the interpreter to translate and explain what had just been read, using Aramaic but following the same pitch and intonation as had been employed by the reader of the original Hebrew. The interpreter was not allowed to refer to a prepared text as he made his comments, since to do so might have misled the congregation into supposing that the translations were authoritative and were to be found in the Torah. In time, however, the translations and comments of the interpreters were collected and recorded. They are called the *Targumim* (translations). The best known is the Targum Onkelos to the Five Books of Moses.

Aramaic as a spoken language has long since passed from the scene, although it is found in our prayer book and extensively also in two books of the Bible, Daniel and Ezra. Yet, until quite recently, while Jews were still living in Yemen and other Arabic countries, synagogues existed where the practice of reading the Targum continued. Even now, there are observant Jews who regularly read at home the weekly Scriptural text twice and the Targum once.

In the synagogue, moreover, the practice of interpreting the Scripture had become too much a part of the service to be dropped. Thus, out of the Targum evolved the *derasha,* a discourse delivered by the *darshan.* It survives today in the sermon delivered by the rabbi. In this way, although the office of darshan has vanished, his function is still carried on.

The Maggid

Among the Ashkenazim, the scholarly commentary by the *darshan* or rabbi was not the only kind of preachment. There was also a sermon by the *maggid*, an itinerant preacher who wandered from place to place, earning a living from the fees or free-will offerings of his listeners. During the nineteenth century and early in the twentieth, the *maggidim* attracted large audiences among the Jews of Russia and Poland, as well as in America, and exerted a strong influence on their listeners.

It may be said that the institution of the *maggid* arose and flourished for the same reason as the Hasidic movement. The masses yearned for a popular interpretation of Judaism which they could understand and appreciate. The *maggid* drew upon the personal experiences of his listeners and by employing similes and imagery he reached the mind and emotions of his audience.

In the Talmudic-Rabbinic period and in the centuries that followed, many rabbis distinguished themselves as great preachers. They drew heavily on the Midrash, a body of Talmudic literature containing Biblical interpretation consisting chiefly of ethical teachings to influence conduct. It comprises legends, folklore, parable and maxims.

During the month of Elul, preceding the High Holy Days and during the Ten Days of Penitence,* when young and old felt the fear of divine judgment approaching, the *maggid* was especially in demand. At this solemn season he reproved the people and strove to arouse his hearers to feelings of contrition, urging them to admit their sins and to call on the Almighty to be forgiven. Every *maggid* had a style of his own. Jacob Kranz, known as the *Maggid* of Dubno, (1740–1804) was perhaps the most renowned and beloved of them all; he was folksy and gentle and noted for his masterly parables. Very different was the Kelmer *Maggid* (1828–1899), so called because he was a native of Kelm, who made his listeners shudder with his description of the torments of Gehenna and eternal damnation. He was a man of great moral stature and a powerful orator. Still other *maggidim* were noted for their logical reasoning. In the United States, Zvi Hirsh Masliansky (1856–1943), a *maggid* of a very high caliber,

*From the first day of the New Year through the Day of Atonement.

was famous during the immigrant period. He preached regularly at the Educational Alliance in New York and was in great demand at Zionist meetings. Whatever approach the *maggidim* took, they heartened their depressed brothers with comforting words and the promise of better days to come. In the climax they voiced the Messianic hope for mankind and Israel. It was customary for a *maggid* to end his discourse with the words *Uva letzion goel*—a redeemer shall come to Zion—to which the people would answer with a fervent "Amen."

The Shamash or Sexton

The literal meaning of *shamash* is "assistant." (The *shamash* candle, for example, is one used to light the other Hanukkah candles.) This officer's duties, as we have noted, are much the same as those that were the *hazzan*'s in Talmudic times. As conditions changed and the *hazzan* became the cantor, his original responsibility for the Torah scrolls and other furnishings of the synagogue were delegated to an assistant.

By the Middle Ages, the *shamash* had acquired a good deal of authority, sometimes acting for the *parnas* or *gabbai* when either of these was absent. It was the *shamash* who assessed taxes and carried out the decisions of the *Bet Din* (rabbinic court)—as, for example, when a public whipping was decreed as a punishment. He or an assistant acted as the *schul klopper*, or public "town crier," going from door to door before a worship service, knocking and calling out that it was soon to begin. There are extant *schul klopper* instruments used by the *shamash*. In smaller communities he also delivered invitations to weddings, circumcisions and other ceremonies. In larger communities he had assistants; in small congregations the offices of *shamash* and *hazzan* and sometimes even rabbi were combined into one.

The Baal Koreh

In certain synagogues today the ritual director—as the *shamash* is also called—serves as the *baal koreh*, or master reader. This function came into existence much as that of the cantor did, as the ability to read and chant the Torah script declined. We have already pointed out the custom for the *hazzan* to stand by the member of the congregation who had been called up to read the Torah, ready to prompt him if he stumbled. As time went on, laymen tended more and more to surrender their prerogative to a professional reader. This was bound to happen as the custom of chanting the Torah developed. In addition to the difficulty of reading the Hebrew script itself, the reader had also to memorize the symbols for the chant, i.e., the *trop*, or cantillation marks, which are printed alongside the text in the printed Bible but not in the Torah scroll. Equally difficult was the reading of the Haftarah, or portion of the prophets—especially in some congregations in which the Haftarah is chanted from scrolls which contain neither vowels nor cantillation marks.

In some synagogues the *baal koreh* is a specially appointed reader. In others, the *hazzan, shamash* or rabbi fulfills this function. In synagogues where the *gabbai*, or lay leader, presides, he stands next to the *baal koreh* while the scriptural portion is chanted. In many reform synagogues, on the other hand, cantillation is a thing of the past; the rabbi simply reads aloud part of the weekly portion. This innovation is one of the departures initiated by the Reform movement thereby eliminating an ancient chant that has through the ages evoked an emotional response from Jewish worshipers.

We have, up to this chapter, discussed the synagogue as essentially a homogeneous institution. When did it become heterogeneous? What brought about the change? Wherein are the present-day synagogues alike and wherein do they differ? Why do they differ? This new development will be presented in the next chapter.

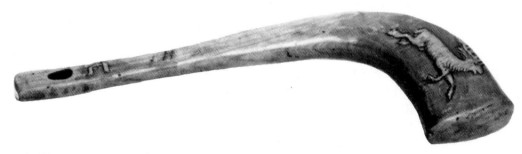

Schulklopper (Hungary 18th Century)

XIII

The Synagogue in a Time of Change: Reform, Conservative, Neo-Orthodox and Reconstructionist Movements

The Rise of Reform

During the nineteenth century, explosive changes in Europe and rapid expansion in America were both reflected in the life of the synagogue. Although most of the thousands of Jews who emigrated from Europe settled in New York and other cities on the eastern seaboard, many caught the heady pioneering spirit of the New World and joined the trek westward. Inland cities such as Pittsburgh and Cincinnati became thriving centers of Jewish life; in 1849, the second year of the California gold rush, there was already a *minyan* for Yom Kippur services in San Francisco.

Meanwhile, at the Beth Elohim Congregation in Charleston an upheaval had taken place that was to have reverberations throughout North America. Like all the earliest congregations, Beth Elohim had been founded by Sephardic Jews. It had strong ties with the synagogues of London and Amsterdam, and its constitution was modeled after theirs. As we have noted, the discipline at a synagogue such as Bevis Marks tended to be strict; it had caused Benjamin Disraeli's father to refuse to serve as warden and later to break away from Judaism entirely. The regulations at Charleston were of the same kind. Whoever desecrated the Sabbath was liable to excommunication. To refuse an office, to be absent from a congregational meeting, to come late, or to attend a *minyan* service not sanctioned by the synagogue trustees made one liable to fines or public humiliation. Every Jew over twenty-one who had lived in Charleston for the period of a year was required to become a member of the congregation. Any Jew who converted, or who married "contrary to Mosaic law," was denied burial in the cemetery unless repentance had been officially declared and accepted at least one year prior to death.

In 1824, forty-seven members of the congregation petitioned for changes in the regulations and also in the liturgy at Beth Elohim. When the petition was not granted, twelve of the forty-seven signers withdrew to organize what they called the "Reformed Society of Israelites." Within two years the dissident group had grown to include fifty families, or about two hundred individual members. This was the beginning of the Reform movement in the New World.

A few years earlier, the first Reform synagogue had been formed in the German city of Hamburg. Whether the revolt in Charleston was entirely spontaneous or had been partly inspired by the German movement is uncertain. At any rate, within a few years the Reverend Gustav Poznanski, a Polish Jew who had ties with the Reform synagogue of Hamburg, was welcomed by the Charleston congregation as its spiritual leader.

European and American Reform

Although the same impulse toward greater freedom from tradition led to the Reform movement on both sides of the Atlantic, the conditions under which it had sprung up in Germany were in some ways quite different. There, as in much of Europe, the *kehillah*—the Jewish communal organization—was recognized and to some degree even supported by the government. Every Jew had to belong to a synagogue in his district or rule himself out as a practicing Jew. The synagogue constitution and appointment of rabbis had to be approved by the state. Even today, synagogues, Jewish day schools and other communal agencies receive legal and financial support from the governments of Denmark, West Germany, Austria, Italy, Holland, Flemish Belgium and the province of Alsace-Lorraine in eastern France. Under such regulations, Jews were assessed by and paid taxes to the *kehillah* which supervised religious education, hospitals, burials, ritual slaughter, and the sale of kosher meat. Births, marriages, and deaths were registered by the *kehillah*. Where this was extant, a Jew who broke away from his congregation was literally cut adrift. In the United States, on the other hand, the separation of church and state applied to the synagogue as well. This meant that circumstances would be less difficult for a Jew who chose to break away, although his social contacts with non-Jews were rather meager, so that he could not expect to have an easy time of it if he separated himself from the congregation.

This was one reason why, in synagogues everywhere, both the force of tradition and the resistance to even the smallest change were so strong. Even in England, where individual Jews had achieved prosperity as well as prestige, their position remained tenuous. To be a member in good standing with one's own congregation was still the one sure way of being socially accepted in the general community and the outside world.

In Germany this kind of pressure was far stronger. Some of its Jewish communities, such as those of Worms and Cologne, dated to the time of the Roman Empire. The pattern of Jewish life there was so bound up with long-established custom and habits of thought that any proposal for change was greeted with horror. Moreover, those who resisted change were strengthened by having the government on their side. Indeed, to those with government authority, any critic or innovator, even in matters of religion, was considered an incipient troublemaker and therefore unwelcome and suspected.

Nevertheless, there were German Jews who believed that change would have to come. They would no longer accept the tradition for keeping the Jewish life style distinct from the people around them. This practice stems from the commandment in Leviticus 18:3, which reads: *Do not copy the practices of Egypt, where you lived, and the practices in Canaan, where I am taking you, nor follow their ways. Follow my regulations, keep my rules. I am the Lord, your God.* They were now too actively "at home" in the world to isolate themselves. They did not feel as comfortable as their forbears had felt with a liturgy that had been little touched by change or revision for a thousand years. They argued that Judaism was a living religion that had developed and changed without going against the Law, and that their own proposals for change were part of its development. They made the cantor (or prayer leader) face the worshiper instead of the Ark. They insisted that it would not really violate the Law to have a prayer book that opened from the right instead of the left, giving prominence to prayers in German. After all, had not the sages declared that *a man may pray in whatever language he desires?* They asked why there should not be organ music on the Sabbath in the synagogue as there was in the church. Were not musical instruments played in the Temple? The prohibition was based, among other reasons, on Leviticus 18:3 and on the verse, *How shall we sing the Lord's song in a strange land* (Psalm 137:4), uttered by the exiles to Babylon. Going still further, they argued that prayers calling down imprecations on the heathen were out of place in modern times, and that the petitions for a return to Zion had lost their meaning and relevance. In the words of Gustav Poznanski when the new Beth Elohim synagogue was dedicated at Charleston in 1841, "This country is our Palestine, this city our Jerusalem, this house of God our Temple."

The debate that began in Hamburg (1818) did not end there and then, but has continued among the Jews to this day. The men who started it had no wish to break entirely with tradition, or from the *kehillah* to which they belonged, to which they paid taxes, and whose benefits they enjoyed. As founders of the Hamburg Temple they continued to be members of the *kehillah* and to acknowledge the authority both of tradition and of Talmudic law, since they were convinced that reform could come only from within. And in time the government agreed to recognize two types of congregations: the Orthodox and the Reform.

In 1845 a much more radical departure, however, was made by the Reform *Gemeinde* (community) of Berlin. Here the length of the prayer book was cut to a total of sixty-four pages in all for the *entire* year; the whole service was translated into German except for the *Shema* and a few other passages; and the weekly service was held on Sunday instead of Saturday morning. This was radical reform indeed and aroused vigorous opposition.

Another reform introduced by the Berlin Reform Congregation was mixed seating for men and women. This idea took root and spread widely. In 1851, family pews were introduced in Anshe Emeth of Albany, N.Y., of which Isaac M. Wise was rabbi. Today in all Reform and in most Conservative congregations, excepting those that are more traditionally oriented, men and women sit and worship together at services. Orthodox congregations adhere to the tradition of separate seating.

But the Reform movement was concerned not only with eliminating the return to Zion, the idea of the Messiah, the resurrection of the dead, or diminishing the emphasis on Hebrew and the sanctity of the Sabbath. On the positive side it called for a more decorous atmosphere during the worship services. As a result, the synagogue became a more formal place. Children under the age of four were not admitted, and parents were held responsible for the behavior of those who were older. The old buzz of gossip and sociable exchange was gone. These were external reforms which eventually Orthodox congregations too would welcome, even though they opposed basic changes in the service itself.

Further regulations put into effect by European Reform pertained to the duties of the rabbi and the cantor, giving them powers that had never before been spelled out in a written document. In some parts of Germany these regulations were enacted as government statutes, with the results that the synagogue became a quasi-state institution, with police power behind it. Although this gave protection of a kind, it also meant that there was less freedom in other ways. For example, individual laymen were now prohibited from calling together a *minyan* for worship without official permission from the *kehillah*. Under their own time-honored law, Jews had had a tradition of being free to assemble for prayer whenever and wherever a *minyan* was organized. Now, however, the state declared it illegal to do so.

In the United States, as we have noted, the separation of church and state made government regulations of this type impossible. Accordingly, each congregation had more freedom to experiment and to make its own regulations without drawing the suspicion of government authorities. Especially was there a spirit of free inquiry and experimentation in communities removed from the eastern seaboard where independence and rugged individualism flourished. It is, therefore, not surprising that the movement that began in Charleston spread to other cities. In 1842 a Reform synagogue was founded in Baltimore; it was followed three years later by Temple Emanu-El in New York City. In 1850, Rabbi Isaac M. Wise told the Orthodox congregation in Albany, to which he had been called, that he did not believe in the coming of the Messiah or the resurrection of the dead. In those days this was heresy. In the uproar that ensued, he was asked to leave the pulpit. As a result of these dramatic events

Temple Emanuel, New York City

a Reform group broke away and formed a temple of its own in Albany. Later Rabbi Wise went to Cincinnati where for fifty years he was preacher, teacher, editor, and chief architect of the Reform movement in the United States. The Hebrew Union College for the training of rabbis, the Central Conference of American Rabbis, and the Union of American Hebrew Congregations grew out of his tireless work as the builder of American Reform.

The Conservative Movement

During a rabbinical conference held in Brunswick, Germany, in 1845, where the above issues were argued and debated, a discussion developed on the use of Hebrew in the synagogue service. Most of the reformers there regarded it as desirable but not legally required. But one member of the group, Rabbi Zechariah Frankel of Dresden, vehemently opposed prayer in the vernacular as well as the deletion of prayers for the return to Zion and Jerusalem. Arguing for moderation according to the modern scientific approach, he urged "conservatism" of traditional Judaism. He withdrew in protest from the militant Reform group and founded a seminary in Breslau, Germany, devoted to working out a midway position between the Orthodox and the Reform. (The latter was led by Abraham Geiger.) This was the beginning of what was to be known as the Conservative movement. In Europe its following remained small and its impact far weaker than that of Reform. Orthodoxy was strong, Reform was young and militant, and there was little opportunity for a middle-of-the-road ideology. But in the New World this new development struck roots and flourished even more than Reform.

The reasons for its success here in America are bound up with events in Europe during the nineteenth century. In Poland and the neighboring countries, the Jewish population had increased to a total of more than a million and a half. But at the same time conditions there had become more and more intolerable. As the central government of Poland collapsed, interference by other governments led to the country's partition by Prussia, Austria, and Czarist Russia, with the largest share going to Russia. In 1795, Poland ceased to exist as a separate kingdom. Meanwhile, the Pale of Settlement had been established in Russia under Catherine the Great, preventing Jews from living in the cities and competing with Russian merchants.

Pogroms, instigated by the Czar, followed. As they grew increasingly savage, the Jews fled in greater and greater numbers to whatever haven they could reach. Many found their way to the United States. By the 1880's more than 20,000 were entering the United States every year; in 1891 alone, the number rose to 100,000. From 1882 to 1914 almost 2,000,000 Jews entered the New World, creating in a few years the largest center of Jewish population in the world—which it still is today.

These new immigrants came from a background quite unlike that of either the Sephardic Jews who had arrived during colonial days or the later arrivals from German and Austrian provinces. The new immigrants came from small communities where Hasidism flourished and where the humble *shtiebel* was generally the house of worship. On New York's Lower East Side, in South Philadelphia, and in similar ghetto communities in other large cities, they would assemble in a rented room to carry on the style of worship they had known in the old country. These transplanted *shtiebels* were a natural gathering place for the natives of a particular hometown, where a newly arrived *landsman* would come in search of old neighbors, a job or for aid and companionship. As they grew more affluent, the immigrant congregations bought former churches and converted them into synagogues of their own. They did not feel comfortable either with the long-established Sephardic congregations or with the German Jews who had become the leaders of the Reform movement. These East European newcomers resented the patronizing attitude of their German coreligionists. They spoke Yiddish rather than German, and had no wish to abandon the old ways in which they felt at home for a ritual in a new language they did not understand.

It was among these people that the Conservative movement won its following. And it was Solomon Schechter who became its acknowledged leader, as Isaac M. Wise had been for American Reform. Born in Eastern Europe, Solomon Schechter came in 1901 to New York, where he was to head the Jewish Theological Seminary. Although his scholarly career had brought him to the University of Cambridge in England and made him famous as the "discoverer" of the *Genizah*, he had never forgotten his early ties with Hasidism and the *shtiebel* of his own childhood. All his life, Judaism remained for him a matter of the heart rather than the head. He believed that Reform was being too rational and intellectual in approach, and that by encouraging assimilation they tended not only to weaken tradition but also to alienate Jews from one another. Moreover, he favored the Zionists, who were working toward a return to the ancient homeland in Palestine—and to this, as has been noted, most Reform leaders in the early years were completely opposed.

The Conservative movement has never clearly defined its position on observance and theology but has left room for adjustment to changing times and circumstances. But realizing, like Isaac M. Wise, that organization was needed, Solomon Schechter proceeded to build the foundations of what in 1913 became the United Synagogues of America. The organization was based on four principles: first, that Judaism constitutes a continuing historical development, neither breaking from nor remaining fixed in the past; second, that it is founded on the Torah; third, that Hebrew is the universal bond of all Jews; and fourth, that although Jews possess a national character, their future does not lie in a secular nationalism, since the Jewish nation exists by virtue of the Torah.

Neo-Orthodoxy

As the debates and controversies raged, Orthodox leaders realized that they too would have to meet the challenge of the new age. Thus arose a new orthodoxy, the Neo-Orthodox movement, led by Rabbi Samson Raphael Hirsch. Hirsch was a German university graduate and a Talmudic scholar, master of the German language and literature, bearer of European culture, and a powerful speaker and writer. Realizing that adjustment to modern ways of life was essential, he introduced an orderly, aesthetic, "aristocratic" type of service with top hats and formal dress wherever possible, black robes for the rabbis, and a beautiful musical service with cantor and male choir. (In some synagogues organ music was played at the services on week days.) He organized an Orthodox school system which was imbued with similar ideals. He taught appreciation of European culture, music and art. He tried to invest the synagogue with dignity, prestige and leadership. But he believed in and preached the Torah as the Supreme Law, revealed by God at Sinai. He stood four-square for the principle of acceptance and obedience to the Tradition. At the same time, he taught his generation of Jews that to be good citizens in the countries where they lived was also a divine obligation.

The difference between Neo-Orthodoxy and the old Orthodoxy

was that the latter shunned, as a rule, contacts with the outside world. It opposed secular learning in public elementary and high schools, colleges and universities. Jewish youth was to spend all their time studying Torah and Talmud. The kind of decorum and aesthetic appointments stressed by the new Orthodoxy were disparaged. In spirit, the old Orthodoxy remained closer to that of the Hasidic *shtiebel*.

The Reconstructionist Movement

From the beginning, the leaders of the American Conservative movement were concerned to see that the synagogue become more than a house of prayer or a house of study. They wanted it to continue to be a neighborhood center as the *shtiebel* had been for the *hasidim* of Eastern Europe. As the pressures from the society around them continued to grow, Jewish leaders began to realize that there must be a conscious effort to make the synagogue a genuinely Jewish social and cultural center. The chief spokesman for this idea was Rabbi Mordecai M. Kaplan, who founded the Jewish Center on the West Side of New York to carry out his ideas. In 1934 he founded Reconstructionism, "the only religious party in Jewish life whose origins are entirely American." He and his disciples composed a new prayer book which reaffirmed the "integrity of worship" by eliminating, adapting, as well as revising (in Hebrew and in English) those parts which are today "intellectually, morally and aesthetically unacceptable." For example, the idea of the Jews being a chosen people, the revelation at Sinai, the resurrection of the dead, the coming of the Messiah, etc., are eliminated in both the Hebrew and the English. They are amended so as to be acceptable to the "modern Jew." However, Reconstructionism advocated worship in Hebrew and the prayers that stress the return to Zion. The Reconstructionists have also taken the radical step of advocating religious equality for women, which among other innovations meant that they may be called up for the reading of the Torah. In keeping with this idea, the Reconstructionists were the first to institute the *bat mitzvah* ceremony to celebrate girls' attaining their religious majority as boys do at bar mitzvah. (The idea and celebration of bat mitzvah, in one form or another, has also been adopted by the Conservative and Reform movements and in Israel.)

Thus, in a country founded on the belief that men should be free to worship as they choose, and that people who are different from one another can still live in freedom and harmony, the history of the synagogue demonstrates that such beliefs can in fact be practiced. It has been a living record of adjustment, of growth and continued vitality, and very different from what the synagogues of Europe were soon to undergo.

XIV

Martyrdom and Rebirth
of the Synagogue

The Incomparable Tragedy

In January 1933, Adolf Hitler became Chancellor of Germany. This
fateful event opened a new chapter of unbelievable horrors in the
history of the Jewish people in Europe and North Africa—and of the
synagogues, educational and communal institutions in these countries, for Jewish destiny has always been inextricably bound with the
synagogue. Hitler's savage armies overran Europe. At his orders, the
Jews began to be "liquidated." Those who could fled to America,
Palestine, England, France or Central and South America—wherever even a temporary refuge could be found. But the majority were
not so fortunate. For them, along the eastern frontier of Germany,
Austria, Poland and all the overrun countries, the death camps were
already prepared and waiting.

The Night of Broken Glass

One of those who managed to escape was Herschl Grynszpan, a
native of Hanover. Using forged documents, he had reached Paris in
1933, when he was twelve years old. His parents, who owned a small
tailor shop, were left behind. Fearful of what was in store for them,
the boy wrote President Roosevelt a desperate plea to allow them to
come to the United States. But even had he received an answer—
which he did not—it was already too late. In November, 1938, a letter
reached him from his parents which had been smuggled out some-
how from a camp in no man's land near the Polish frontier. They had

159

been brought there in a cattle truck, which they had been forced to board at bayonet point. All around the camp were fields enclosed with barbed wire, where the people were dying of typhus or starvation, or going mad. Stables and pigsties were their only shelters.

Half crazed by the news, Herschl bought a revolver and went to the German embassy. He demanded an interview at once. When a third secretary named Ernst von Rath appeared, Herschl fired five shots into his body. He then gave himself up, declaring, "We are not dogs!"

The assassination became the pretext for wave upon wave of Nazi propaganda. At a celebration in Munich, the shooting was described as part of an international Jewish plot, and was therefore exploited as the signal for new pogroms. That infamous night, November 9, 1938, has gone down in history as the *Kristallnacht*, the Night of Broken Glass. All over Germany, synagogues were attacked and vandalized. A total of one hundred ninety-one were set afire; seventy-six were completely destroyed. Among the latter was the venerable synagogue of Worms, a landmark that had survived almost a thousand years. Fastened to the ruins of each gutted building was a sign that read: *Revenge for the Murder of Vom Rath. Death to International Jewry.*

Blitzkrieg, Bombing—and Reconstruction

Less than a year later, after a series of impotent, futile, cowardly negotiations, Europe was at war. The beginning of the Tragedy came with the Nazi invasion of Poland. As noted in the foregoing chapter, the kingdom of Poland had ceased to exist after the partition that took place toward the end of the eighteenth century. It was revived at the peace conference following the war of 1914–1918. Now, just over twenty years later, it was again obliterated. The events of the first weeks of September 1939 brought a new word into the language —*blitzkrieg*, or "lightning war." When Hitler's armored divisions rolled eastward, looting and burning as they went, the fate of the three million Jews of Poland was sealed. And the doom of the people was shared by their houses of worship. All through Poland, all through the Baltic countries of Lithuania, Latvia and Estonia, and in the Russian Pale of Jewish Settlement, synagogues that had not been burned or otherwise destroyed were converted into stables or ware-

New Great Synagogue of Strasbourg

Old Great Synagogue (1898–1940) Strasbourg, France

houses. The modest wooden synagogues of Polish towns, and those built of stone—part fortress and part house of worship—which had risen in the turbulent years of the seventeenth century, were wiped out never to rise again. All that we have left to-day is a memorial book of photographs, *Wooden Synagogues,* by Maria and Kazimierz Piechotka.*

The bombing raids of the war brought destruction also to synagogues in England, Holland and Italy. One of those badly damaged was the Tempio Grande of Padua, Italy, which had been dedicated in 1683. There was desecration of these sacred edifices too. One of the most beautiful buildings to suffer this fate was the synagogue of Florence, with its rich decoration of Venetian mosaics. Used by occupying German troops as a warehouse, it was partly destroyed by them when they were forced to retreat. After the war it was rebuilt with the financial assistance of the Italian government, the American Jewish Joint Distribution Committee, and the Conference of Jewish Material Claims Against Germany.† To-day it is designated as a national Italian monument.

Elsewhere in Europe, the pattern has been the same. Small groups of survivors—embers snatched from the flames of the holocaust—banded together to rebuild and rehabilitate the communities ravaged by the war. With the help of funds from Jewish institutions, the sale of community assets as well as financial aid from provincial and city governments, they built compounds that included not only synagogues but also housing for the pitiful remnants as well as clinics and special homes for the aged. Many of these buildings serve as living monuments to communities that were totally exterminated. In Hamburg and West Berlin, the rebuilt synagogue centers have incorporated features of those that were destroyed. The largest of the reconstructed synagogues is in Strasbourg, France. Built in the traditional basilica style, with twelve sixty-foot columns supporting its roof, it seats 1700 people and includes a weekday chapel, a library, classrooms and meeting halls. Nearby is a special building housing a religious day-school.

---

*Arkady Publishers, Warsaw, 1959.
†The floods of 1960 severely damaged the synagogue once again, but it has since been restored.

Synagogue, Florence, Italy

Interior of Synagogue

Converted Synagogues

We have already noted (see Chapter IX) that two synagogue structures in medieval Spain escaped destruction only by having been
converted into churches. This was true in other parts of Europe as
well. In the Moslem countries of North Africa and the Middle East,
many synagogues underwent a similar fate of conversion into
mosques. Equally sad, the more because it affected the world's largest Jewish center in recent years, has been the desecration that took
place following the Russian Revolution of 1917. Following the collapse first of Czarist rule and then of the revolutionary provisional
government, the Bolsheviks seized power. The result was civil war,
with the worst of the fighting concentrated in the region of the
Ukraine, including the old Pale of Settlement. Here, as in Poland, it
was the Jews who suffered most. The number who died was at least
100,000, and may have been as high as a quarter of a million.

Since the victorious Communist government is officially and ag-
gressively atheistic, Jews have found it increasingly impossible to
worship or observe Jewish ceremonies and rituals, such as the circumcision of boys, the study of Hebrew, the ceremony of bar mitzvah
and so on. Nor can they maintain contacts with world Jewry. Along
with churches the synagogues, whose attendance diminished, were
closed by decree and were converted into club houses and recreation
centers. Under similar regulations, the writing of Torah scrolls, the
printing of prayer books, and the training of rabbis, cantors, *mohelim*
(those qualified to circumcise) and *shochtim* (ritual slaughterers)
have practically disappeared, and Jewish life, with the synagogue as
its center, is being all but starved out of existence.

More recently, anti-Semitism has appeared once again in the
Soviet Union. The same is true of Poland. The latter, as was pointed
out, due to the enlightened policy of its Christian kings had become
the liveliest center of Jewish life and culture in all of Europe. The
Nazi invasion and the death camps reduced the total of Poland's
Jewish population from three million to 250,000. The campaign of
annihilation that burned the synagogues and destroyed hundreds of
communities drove tens of thousands of Polish Jews into the Warsaw
ghetto, where they lived crowded together, struggling against cold,
disease and starvation. They had totaled half a million in October
1940; but deportations to the extermination camps had reduced their
number by May 1943 to about 40,000. The story of the resistance by

those who remained, fighting on for weeks, from house to house, and finally from bunker to bunker, against the Nazi troops who attempted to subdue them, is one of the most heroic in the history of the Jews. The few who escaped through the sewers of the ghetto joined with the partisans of the Polish underground in the fight against the Nazis. Yet despite this heroism, beginning with 1946 the Poles repeatedly turned on the remaining Jews with new waves of persecutions and pogroms which cut their number to a mere fraction. Today this creative, glorious Jewish world center is no more.*

New Beginnings in Israel

Long before the war, a growing number of Jews had realized that there was no future for Jewish life and religion in Europe, and had turned their hopes once again toward Eretz Israel. This is the theme of *The Messenger from the Holy Land,* a short story by S. Y. Agnon, the first writer in Hebrew to win the Nobel Prize for literature (1966). The story is a fantasy of how a synagogue in Poland miraculously transported itself, Torah scrolls, Ark, *bimah,* books and all, to the Holy Land.

During the early years of the twentieth century, increasing numbers of pioneers had migrated to Palestine to do the hard work of building a new life there. In 1948, after a fierce and bitter struggle, military as well as political, the modern state of Israel was born. Its founders had come from Russia, Poland, Germany and the nations of Eastern Europe, as well as countries such as Italy with its relatively small Jewish population, Moslem countries and from the Western Hemisphere.

Transplanted Synagogues

Until about the middle of the nineteenth century, the Jews of Italy had been scattered throughout more than a hundred towns, many of them small in numbers. Then a movement to the major cities began, chiefly to Rome, Milan and Florence where more than two-thirds of the 30,000 remaining Italian Jews now live. In the central Italian

*Similar destruction, ruin and conversion have been the lot of the synagogues in the Jewish communities of North Africa, Egypt, Syria, Iraq and all Moslem countries except Iran and possibly Morocco.

Burning of Oranienburg Synagogue, Berlin, November 9, 1938

NIEMALS WIEDER

KRISTALLNACHT

1938

10

DDR

BERLIN W8

8.11.63.-10

R MAHNUNG
AN DIE
LLNACHT 1938

*East German postage stamp memorializing Nazi
atrocities (note the burning of a synagogue, the
yellow star and the slogan to the left,* Never Again)

*Reconstructed Berlin-Charlottenburg Jewish Community House and Syna-
gogue* (Photo: Karl and Helma Tölle)—*note the remains of the old building
built into the new*

town of Mantua, for example, the Jewish population in 1900 numbered two thousand; today it is less than two hundred. The Jewish community in the neighboring village of Sermide which dated back five hundred years, had meanwhile dwindled to a handful and was altogether extinguished in 1936, when its last surviving member died.

In 1940 a group of Italian-born Jews emigrated to Jerusalem, where they formed a congregation. In 1952, thanks to the efforts of their *parnas*, Dr. Shlomo Nahon, the fantasy of the synagogue in Agnon's story became a fact, as all the furnishings of the beautiful little synagogue of Conegliano Veneto*—which had been closed for fifty years—were transported to Jerusalem as a gift from the Jewish community of Venice. Restored and refurnished, the *Aron Kodesh*, the *bimah*, the pews, the paneling and the lattice-work of the women's gallery have made the new building they adorn one of the most picturesque houses of worship in Jerusalem.

Transporting these furnishings from Conegliano Veneto marked the beginning of a movement that brought many sanctuaries, after years of neglect and decay, to a new life in Israel. The Italian Jewish communities donated the relics, with the permission of the Italian government, and the Israeli Ministry of Religious Affairs paid the cost of dismantling, packing and shipping them. Perhaps the most venerable of the treasures that made the journey was the *Aron Kodesh* of San Daniele del Friuli. It had been carved by a Jewish craftsman, Nathaniel Luzzatto, not long after the founding of the synagogue in this north Italian village in the year 1400.

In 1955 the *Aron Kodesh* of the Tempio Grande of Padua, which had been badly damaged by an air raid in 1943, was dismantled piece by piece and transferred to Tel Aviv, where it now stands in the synagogue of a suburb, Yad Eliahu. The dwindling of the ancient Jewish community at Padua—which now consists of less than two hundred persons—led to the abandonment of another synagogue, the Tempio Spagnolo, whose Ark had been completed and dedicated in 1733. The Ark now stands in the synagogue of Hekhal Shlomo, the supreme religious center in Jerusalem. The Israel Museum in Jerusalem houses an old Italian synagogue. Other synagogues have been transplanted to various settlements. Torah scrolls, too, have been

*Erected early in the eighteenth century.

Pilgrimage to the tomb of Shimon ben Yohai, Meron, Galilee

Hekhal Shlomo: Israel Supreme Religious Center

transported. Recently, with the approval and cooperation of the Rumanian government, hundreds of Torah scrolls from Rumanian synagogues have been shipped to Israel synagogues. Thus, the *aliya* (immigration) of synagogues and Torah scrolls continues.

More than anywhere else in the world, the Jews of Israel keep alive the memory of the victims of the Nazis and the towns destroyed by them. This is reflected in the large number of synagogues named after communities wiped out by the holocaust. With a few notable exceptions such as those just mentioned, these are modest buildings reminiscent of the *shtiebels* of Eastern Europe.

Sacred Shrines

From time immemorial, shrines have existed at the burial places of famous rabbis and at sites connected with ancient tradition, such as, for example: the reputed tomb of King David on Mount Zion in Jerusalem, Rachel's tomb in Bethlehem, Elijah's cave near Haifa, and the cave of the Patriarchs at Hebron, to mention a few of the best known. Jews have always come there to worship, to light memorial candles for the departed, to express earnest and humble prayers for healing and aid or just to visit.

Of all the monuments revered by Jews, the one most visited is undoubtedly the Western Wall in Jerusalem which is never free of worshipers. No one who has witnessed it can forget the Sukkot celebration with the palm branches and *etrogim* (citrus fruits), or the *Tisha B'Av* lamentations and other occasions. Equally stirring is the sight of students dancing, arms interlocked, as they descend from the heights where their yeshivahs are located, to welcome Queen Sabbath at the Friday evening services. Each season of the year is filled with a succession of appropriate moving events at this ancient beloved site. Here Jews of the most diverse social and ethnic origins bring their Torah scrolls to pray side by side, each group according to its own special ritual.

Of the various ceremonies performed at Har Zion, the one that is richest in drama and symbolism takes place at the beginning of the Sukkot festival once every seven years, to observe the *shemitah*, the year in which—according to the regulation in Leviticus, Chapter 25 —the fields are to lie fallow. Heading a procession of worshipers carrying the *etrog* (citron) and *lulav* (palm branch) are seventy elders, each representing an ethnic group (such as Yemenite, Bokha-

Sukkot service at the Western Wall, Jerusalem

ran, Kurdistani, etc.) that has settled in Israel, and each carrying a taper which is lighted on the ascent to Mount Zion.

Of the annual pilgrimages outside Jerusalem, probably the most famous takes place on *Lag B'Omer,* when thousands make the journey north to the grave of Simon Bar Yohai at Meron and there participate in colorful ceremonies that continue through the night.

Youth Synagogues

In the one country in the world where the Jews are not a minority people, it is not surprising that the synagogues have a special character. The welfare of Jewish citizens is no longer the responsibility of a community organization but of the national government. For this and other reasons, the Israel synagogue's functions, as compared with congregations in the rest of the world, are limited to worship, adult study of the Jewish heritage, religious ceremonies such as bar mitzvah, and the like.

A tendency peculiar to modern Israel has been the rapid establishment of separate youth synagogues. In the recent past, and in some communities even now, such a movement flourished in the United States, where it was known as Young Israel. In fact, Israel's young people are creating a new kind of synagogue, one that will reflect *their* life and *their* outlook as native-born Israelis. Unencumbered by nostalgia for the life their parents left behind in the *galut* (Diaspora), they are rather impatient with the ethnic rituals and customs of the old folks. As in any movement for change, there is continuous dialogue and debate about the Old World practices and chants and the part they should play in Israel today—a debate that is becoming academic as new youth synagogues are established, modernizing the Israeli life style. Another peculiarly Israeli development is taking place in the *kibbutzim.* Although the members in these rural collectives are as a rule non-observant and even non-religious, they have built modest synagogues for their parents and for other older people who have come to join them from the Old World. It is the hope of every believer in historic Judaism that the influence of the grandparents who take their sabra grandchildren to worship in these synagogues will be, in the words of the prophet Malachi (3:24) to *turn the heart of the fathers to the children, and the heart of the children to their fathers.*

An Historic Sabbath

The struggle of the Jews to re-establish a homeland in Zion has been going on for almost two thousand years. What it meant to translate so old a hope into reality is suggested by a passage from the memoirs of a British statesman and Jewish leader, Sir Herbert Samuel, who in 1920 was sent by England to serve as High Commissioner of Palestine. He thus became the first Jewish governor of the Holy Land since the year 70 C. E. Of his first Sabbath there, he wrote:

> The most moving ceremony that I have ever attended was on my first visit, after my arrival in Jerusalem, to the old and spacious synagogue in the Jewish quarter of the ancient city.* As it was the Sabbath, I had walked over from Government House so as not to offend the Orthodox by driving, and found the surrounding streets densely thronged, and the great building itself packed to the doors and to the roof, mostly by older settlers, some of those who had come to live, and to die, in the Holy City for piety's sake. Now, on that day, for the first time since the destruction of the Temple, they could see one of their own people as governor in the Land of Israel. To them it seemed that the fulfillment of ancient prophecy might at last be at hand. When, in accordance with the usual ritual, I was "called to the Reading of the Law," and from the central platform recited in Hebrew the prayer and the blessing, *Have mercy upon Zion, for it is the home of our life, and save her that is grieved in spirit, speedily, even in our days. Blessed art Thou, O Lord, who makest Zion joyful through her children;* and when (I read) the opening words of a chapter of Isaiah appointed for that day, *Comfort ye, comfort ye my people, saith your God. Speak ye comfortingly to Jerusalem, and cry unto her, that her warfare is accomplished, that her iniquity is pardoned*—the emotion that I could not but feel seemed to spread throughout the vast congregation. Many wept. One could almost hear the sigh of generations. . . .**

*the so called Hurvah Synagogue, the largest Ashkenazie edifice.
**Herbert Samuel, *Memoirs*, London, Curtis Brown, 1945, p. 176.

Synagogue on the Hebrew University Campus, Jerusalem, named after Rabbi Israel Goldstein

Desecration and Reconstruction in Old Jerusalem

During the Israel War of Independence of 1948, the Jordanian Arabs seized East or Old Jerusalem, bringing desecration and destruction to all but one of its thirty-five ancient synagogues, as well as to Talmudic academies and the Jewish cemetery on the Mount of Olives. Hundreds of precious ancient books and scrolls were seized and burned. Houses of worship and study that were not razed to the ground were converted for use as chicken houses, stables, and refuse dumps. Tombstones were uprooted, broken into pieces, and used as paving stones for houses, yards, army barracks—and even latrines.

In June, 1967, when Israel again took possession of Old Jerusalem, it soon learned that the destruction and profanation had been worse than anyone had previously supposed. Elie Eliachar, native son and deputy mayor of Jerusalem, reminisces in his memoirs* on the four ancient Sephardic synagogues which he frequented as a child. One, named the Rabban Yohanan ben Zakkai, rebuilt by the Spanish Jewish exiles, was believed to have been located on the site of the academy built by the great teacher who ensured the future of Jewish life by establishing Yavneh as the center of rabbinic study and the seat of the Sanhedrin. It was here that the British High Commissioner, Sir Herbert Samuel, would pray occasionally. Around it were the synagogues of Elijah the Prophet, another called "Stamboul," and connecting all four, the Central Synagogue. Each was a distinct and separate entity. In addition to this complex there were other synagogues nearby. Outstanding were the Rabbi Yehuda Ha-Hasid, called the *Hurvah*, or Ruin, originally built in 1700, and the Cabbalist Bet-El Synagogue. Happily, these synagogues are now being rebuilt. But gone forever are the "exquisite furnishings" and ancient ornaments which decorated them, according them a unique charm. Especially missed is the "Chair of Elijah"—which stood near the house of worship bearing his name—on which infant boys were circumcised. From this chair Elijah was to proclaim the redemption of Zion. Also lost were the "Bridegroom's Chair," where the groom sat in his place of honor before being led to the bride's house, the jar of oil and a *shofar* for heralding the coming of the Messiah and his anointment.

Like many medieval synagogues, especially the Sephardic, these

*"Old Jerusalem Synagogues", *Jewish Spectator,* March 1971.

A desecrated synagogue (all that is left is a Hebrew inscription)

too were below street level. As stated earlier, some explain this was to observe the intent of the prayer, *From the depths have I cried unto Thee* (Ps. 130, 1) and *Who remembered us in our low estate* (Ps. 136, 23). Another, more realistic explanation is that it was the result of the Jews' compromise with the Moslem injunction (similar to that of the Christian in Europe) forbidding the erection of such structures at a point higher than or as high as mosques. Since Moslems revered Elijah (childless Moslem women light oil lamps in his honor and pray to him to bless them with offspring), the Arabs did not destroy the Sephardic synagogue as completely as they had the others. The thick walls, vaulted ceilings, and windows and arches left standing now serve as the frame on which the old synagogues are being rapidly reconstructed.

The day of June 7, 1967, will assuredly remain as historic a date as any mentioned in the preceding chapters. The restoration to Israel of the most precious possessions of the Jewish people—such as *Ha'-Kotel Ha'Maaravi* (the Western Wall), Rachel's Tomb in Bethlehem, the Cave of Machpellah in Hebron—have thrilled Jews all over the world. Enshrined in the Jewish hearts and minds they have opened up new vistas for religious expression and creativity.

The rebuilding of the ruined historic synagogues in Old Jerusalem is a cause for rejoicing among young and old. The outpouring of concern and love that has resulted in the decision to rehabilitate these age-old hallowed sites not only is indicative of the emotions of the present but constitute an inspiration for the future. They are symbols of a united people and herald great things yet to come.

XV

The Contemporary Synagogue, Synagogue Customs, Ornaments and Objects

Many Faces of the Synagogue

The synagogue in the past, as in the present, has been in the very center of Jewish life, not only religiously and spiritually, but also socially and economically. It has been the focus, pivot and motor force of other institutions. Even before the ghetto was imposed on them, Jews habitually sought to cluster together in one section of the town—around the synagogue. It was not only the place where they prayed and studied but the community "home" where they lived and felt most comfortable. Personal joys and sorrows were shared and reflected in the service by special prayers. It met their needs in times of distress and joy, in normal as well as in critical periods.

What is more, like one's home, the synagogue varied its appearance with the seasons. During the High Holy Days it was a very solemn place. On Purim it was a scene of frivolity, the children deafening the congregation with the tumult of *Haman klappers*, graggers and all types of ingenious noise-makers whenever Haman's name was pronounced during the reading of the Scroll of Esther. Purim was a day of free-for-all when congregants impersonated the rabbi and the dignitaries, poking fun at them. (Indeed, the birth of the Jewish theatre is traced to the Purim *spiel* (play).

In the Hasidic *shtiebel* on the last day of Passover the congregants enacted in song and dance the crossing of the Red Sea by pouring water on the floor. On Shavuot the prayer hall was decorated with flowers and greens, while on Tisha B'av it resembled a mourner's home, with the lights dimmed and people sitting on or close to the ground. In contrast, on the festival of *Simhat Torah* (Rejoicing in the Law), there were tumultuous "circuits," Torah scroll processions with paper flags, burning candles and boisterous play-acting celebrations which overflowed into the streets. On this day of merriment it was a *mitzvah* (precept) to become tipsy at the sumptuous *kiddush* (reception) given respectively by the *Bridegroom of the Torah* (the man honored by being called up for the very last section of the reading from the scroll) and of *Bereshith* (the man honored by being called to begin the very first section, *In the Beginning*). On Sabbath mornings, after the bar mitzvah boy or the bridegroom completed the chanting of the *Haftarah* (prophetic portion), a shower of almonds and raisins descended on the congregants.

When newly bereaved children and blood relatives were admitted publicly to the congregational worship at a certain point in the Friday evening service with the words, *May the Lord comfort you*, or when the members of the congregation joined them in reciting the *kaddish* (prayer for the dead), the individuals concerned experienced the reality of his membership in the family of Israel.

The synagogue was indeed a second home.

Women and Children

As indicated, until the advent of Reform Judaism the sexes were separated; women worshiped in rooms at the side or above the men's synagogue, keeping in touch with the men's service through a small opening, lattice or partition called *mehitzah*. They were frequently led by competent women officiants, who synchronized with the cantor or Torah-reader during the service, often adding a running commentary to the Bible reading. Thus, the synagogue was the school where every Jewish woman received informal instruction on how to conduct a Jewish home and raise her children. As indicated, this separate section was known as the *ezrat nashim* (women's section).

Although children are troublesome because they make it difficult to keep order, they too were given attention and consideration. On *Simhat Torah* those under thirteen years of age are called to ascend the *bimah* for a special children's *aliyah*. Very impressive, then as now, is the sight of children huddled under a large *tallit* (prayer shawl), reciting the blessings of the Torah as the *baal koreh* chants the text. They take part in the procession of the Torah scrolls

Temple Beth Sholom, Elkins Park, Pennsylvania (designed by Frank Lloyd Wright), built of glass and plastic panels (Photo: Jacob Stelman)

around the prayer hall. They stand by the steps of the *bimah* and reverently kiss the scrolls before these are returned to the Ark. They are privileged to sip from the wine cup at the end of the Sabbath evening and morning services when the *kiddush* (sanctification of the wine) is recited by the cantor.

Those under thirteen carried their father's prayer books, Bible and *tallit*-sack to "schul." And to this day, at Sephardic services, the sight of the head of the family enveloping his children and grandchildren under the canopy of his *tallit* as the cantor sings out the threefold priestly blessing (Numbers 6:24–27) is unforgettable.

Regulations as to Building and Public Worship

The architecture of the synagogue building was not restricted. Generally the buildings were oblong, although some were octagonal, circular or square. They were ornate or unpretentious, depending on the community. Their orientation had to be toward Jerusalem which, for the large majority of communities, was eastward. One requirement was universal: that it have windows, preferably twelve, to equal the number of the tribes, and that it be well lit. In this respect the prophet Daniel (6:11) was followed: *His windows were open. . . . toward Jerusalem and he kneeled upon his knees three times a day and prayed and gave thanks before his God* (Daniel 6:11). The Talmud in *Berachot* 34b warns against praying in a room without windows. Rashi comments that windows are needed so that those at prayer can see the sky and be inspired to an attitude of worship. The *Halakhah* (Law) went still further, in saying that there should be *twelve* windows (probably to represent the twelve tribes). Although the latter requirement was not always met, all synagogues do have windows. As to other aspects of the structure, they reflected the environment. The floors, for example, in Mediterranean and Oriental countries, were made of stone. Many synagogue interiors left a conspicuous portion of the wall, usually facing the entrance, unplastered or unpainted, to remind the worshipers of the destruction of Jerusalem and the Temple.

Whenever possible, a vestibule was built in front of the main sanctuary so that the house of worship was not entered directly from the street. This, as one distinguished rabbi explained, was meant to provide the worshiper with an opportunity of shedding the worldly atmosphere of the street and marketplace before entering the house of prayer. In many old synagogue vestibules and in the *shtiebels* there was at the entrance, a water outlet of some kind for washing the hands, and in Moslem lands even for washing the feet.

It was also mentioned that any ten Jews who have reached the religious majority may organize a synagogue. The word *minyan* (the quorum of ten required) means number. In some small communities a rotating "recruitment" system is followed to assure a *minyan*; in others, payment is arranged for "professionals" to maintain the minimum required for public worship. These are sometimes called the *assarah batlanim* (ten "idlers" or leisurely persons).

Praying with the congregation makes the worshiper feel at one with the hopes, ideas and ideals of his people. It links the individual with his forbears and ancestors. It helps him identify as a member of a people that extends world-wide both physically and spiritually. Under its influence his attachment to the Jewish people becomes strengthened and more meaningful.

Synagogue Furnishings

Through the ages, the furnishings of the synagogue have varied in outward appearance and location; otherwise they have remained almost unchanged. The most important of these furnishings is, of course, the *Aron Kodesh*, the Holy Ark in which the Torah scrolls are kept. Originally a portable chest, it later became the ornately carved and decorated Ark we know today, the most conspicuous object in any synagogue. Next in importance is the *bimah*, the table for the cantor and for the reading of the Scriptures. There may also be a stand or lectern, known as the *amud*, for the cantor and rabbi. In ancient times the *bimah* stood before the Ark, where the leader conducted the service with his face toward the Ark and his back to the congregation. Later, it became customary to place the *bimah** at the center of the hall—a position it still occupies in traditional synagogues today. In most synagogues it is now placed at the front, to one side of the Ark, so that the reader stands facing the congregation. (In the latter part of the last century and early in this century the placing of the *bimah* was

*While it is a feature of the Sephardic and many Orthodox synagogues, it has all but disappeared in American synagogues.

a source of grave controversy.) The *bimah* is usually situated on a
raised platform so as to make it easier for the worshipers to see the
leader and thus to follow the service.

Suspended over the Holy Ark in many synagogues which follow
the Ashkenazi ritual is a *parokhet,* a beautifully wrought curtain
adapted from the veil used in the sanctuary. Sephardic synagogues
suspend it inside the Ark. Hanging before the Ark is the *ner tamid,*
or perpetual light. Like so many things about the synagogue, it has
a scriptural origin, viz., the instruction given to Aaron in Exodus
27:20–21:

> You shall further instruct the Israelites to bring you pure olive
> oil . . . to cause a lamp to burn continually. Aaron and his sons
> shall set it up in the Tent of Meeting, outside of the parokhet
> which is over the Tablets to burn before the Lord. Thus shall it
> be for all time . . .

In addition, the synagogue is usually lighted by a menorah or
candelabrum, to memorialize the Temple and to perpetuate the
injunction never to forget it. Although Jews were enjoined not to use
replicas of the seven-branched menorah after the destruction of the
Temple (as a sign of mourning), this practice has not been always
observed.

Each of the furnishings of the synagogue enjoys a priority rank
in order of holiness which must be maintained and never reduced.
This order begins, of course, with the Torah scroll, which because it
contains the name of God is sacred. The sanctity of all other furnishings and objects is based on the degree of their proximity—in space
and in use—to the Sefer Torah itself. Thus, for example, an old *Aron
Kodesh* may not be cut down and made into a bench on which the
Torah scroll is placed—although to do the opposite would be permitted.

The Uses and Ownership of the Synagogue

Degrees of holiness also apply to the synagogue building itself. One
used as a house of study *(bet midrash)* is regarded as holier than one
used as a house of assembly *(bet knesset),* again because of the holiness conferred by the study of the Torah. For this reason, although

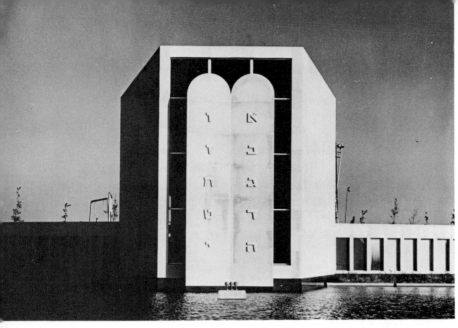

International Synagogue at the J. F. Kennedy Airport, New York City

Air Force Jewish Chapel, Colorado Springs, Colorado

a house of assembly may be converted into a house of study, the reverse is not permitted. The rule applies even though some of the regulations governing a *bet midrash* are less strict than for a *bet knesset;* for example, teachers and students may be allowed to eat and sleep in the former in order to allow more time for their studies.

On the other hand, the traditional regulations forbid using the upper stories of a synagogue building as a dwelling. This applies only to buildings constructed for the express purpose of worship; like many other regulations, they had to be relaxed when a private house was used as a synagogue. Among other such regulations, the *Shulhan Arukh* (Code of Laws) lists the following that are forbidden in a synagogue: one may not use it as a regular place for eating, drinking or sleeping; engaging in business (other than that concerned with charity or the redemption of captives); as a shelter from the heat or cold; as a place for idle talk or gossip, and the like. A worshiper was permitted to enter with his stick or satchel but he was required to clean the mud from his shoes before entering. He could not enter carrying a knife with an exposed blade.

Unless specific conditions had been made at the time of building, all these regulations were to apply even after the synagogue had become a ruin. Even then it was to be treated reverently.

The synagogue was to be owned by the community and by those who had contributed toward building it. If an individual built a synagogue for private worship he was not to keep out any Jew from worshiping in it. As with any public property, difficulties have often arisen over the question of whether and how a synagogue is to be sold. In a small town, where there have been no donations from outsiders and where the synagogue is rarely used by strangers, the decision to sell can easily be made at a general meeting of residents or their chosen representatives. In a city, however, things are less simple. It is often hard to find out whether strangers have contributed toward the cost of the building, and to sell it without their permission would mean depriving them of what in part is rightfully theirs. The *Halakhah* suggests some ways of dealing in advance with this problem—as, for example, by assigning the responsibility for such a decision to a specific rabbi at the time of building, or by specifying that the spiritual leader of the congregation, whoever he might be at the time of the proposed sale, be given the power to decide. These regulations are especially relevant nowadays as Jews evacuate old neighborhoods and dispose of their houses of worship.

Traditional regulations forbid the demolition of a synagogue unless another building has already been put up to replace it, thus guarding against possible delay in completing a new building. This is to apply, however, only so long as the first synagogue is still usable; if it is in a state of deterioration and in danger of collapse, it may be demolished before the rebuilding of another is begun.

Other regulations apply to the breaking away of part of a congregation to build a new synagogue. If such a move becomes absolutely necessary—and the rabbis say that every effort should be made to avoid this—the sacred objects are to be divided between the two congregations in proportion to their membership. Anyone who donates an object to the synagogue has the right to have it inscribed in his name. Inscriptions may be made only in the name of the person who donates the money or the person who did the work, if such work represented a donation. On the other hand the name of a person may not be inscribed at whose initiative or during whose term of office there have been alterations or extensions of the building.

Seating Arrangements

Even though the synagogue is the property of the entire congregation, custom and prestige have a way of allowing members to establish special claims in the seating arrangements of the synagogue. We have seen in Chapter XI how during the early days of Shearith Israel, a "lady *parnas*" of the congregation grew so attached to her own seat of honor that she refused to give it up.

Much the same situation existed in the Old World too. *The World of Sholom Aleichem**—a book on the life of the *shtetl*, the townlet that is the place of origin for many Jews living in America today—contains a chapter entitled "A Seat by the Eastern Wall." It tells of identical twin brothers whose father, though poor, was a scholar and an honored citizen. When he died, the only inheritance he left them was a seat close to the Holy Ark at the *Mizrach* (eastern wall), which as everyone knew was the place of honor and prestige. This pew had been handed down from father to son for generations. The story recounts the "shameful events" that followed the period

*Maurice Samuel, New York, Alfred A. Knopf, 1943.

of mourning, told as only the master storyteller, Sholom Aleichem, could have told it. The origin of the customs that could lead to such quarrels can probably be traced to a regulation in the *Shulhan Aruch,* providing that elders were to sit facing the congregation. Later on, it seems to have become customary for those who had contributed to the building and furnishing of the synagogue to occupy a seat of honor. Indeed since the sale of pews was a substantial source of income, they were regarded as part of the estate of the contributors.

The Contemporary Synagogue

Concerning another pair of twins, whose rivalry is described in the Book of Genesis, the rabbis have a story of their own. They explain that when Rebekah was pregnant with Jacob and Esau, the unborn twins were already struggling in her womb. Why did they struggle? According to the story, when she passed a house of study, Jacob tried to emerge, and when she passed a place of heathen worship, it was Esau who struggled to get out. Evidently the rabbis found it hard to imagine a time when there had not been a synagogue.

All through its long history, another kind of struggle has gone on within the synagogue itself—the struggle between the pressure for change and the stabilizing force of tradition. The results of the pressure for change are especially notable in the synagogue of today. The most striking of these results has been the development of the Reform, Conservative, Neo-Orthodox and Reconstructionist movements, described in Chapter XIII. Others will be evident to anyone who has ever visited a military chapel or the International Synagogue at the John F. Kennedy Airport in New York, erected in 1967.

To meet the needs of the armed forces, multipurpose interfaith chapels have been set up. In Israel, a synagogue travels with the military forces, and is usually housed in a tent under a camouflage cover. A specially constructed *Aron Kodesh* goes with it, equipped with a small Torah scroll, along with a *shofar,* Sabbath candlesticks, *kiddush* cup, prayer shawls and phylacteries. The *Aron Kodesh* is equipped with handlebars so that it can be carried by two men, much as the Ark of the Covenant was carried through the desert of Sinai. To Orthodox soldiers, the very act of transporting it brings to mind the scriptural verse in Deutoronomy 23:15: *Since the Lord your God*

Jewish soldiers in a Thanksgiving Service after U.S. troops crossed the German Siegfried Line (1944). Note the "dragons' teeth" obstructions

moves about in your camp to protect you and to deliver your enemies to you, let your camp be holy. Moreover, special prayers and a uniform liturgy, acceptable to the diverse ethnic groups, have been composed for the Israel Armed Forces. Thus, in the land that inspired the birth of the synagogue, the forces of change and of tradition have again found a way of meeting and joining hands. In the United States during World War II, special revolving chapels were designed to accommodate the three major faiths—Jewish, Protestant and Catholic—represented in the United States Armed Forces. The use of rollers, a circular platform, and a rotating table makes it possible to adapt these chapels easily to the worship of each group. In fact, this same idea has been adopted at some universities. In others, for example, at Brandeis in Waltham, Massachusetts, a cluster of three chapels has been constructed as an acknowledgment both of the existence of a common Judeo-Christian heritage and of the differences within it. At the aforementioned John F. Kennedy International Air Terminal in New York, there is also a cluster of three chapels to accommodate air travelers who wish to worship before or after landing, as well as the personnel of the airfield. It is probably the only synagogue that is welcome to Jews of every shade of belief, from the Hasidic to the Reform.

The Suburban Synagogue

Among recent developments in response to change, none is more conspicuous than the growth in the United States of the suburban Jewish center. It came with the end of the Second World War, as more and more Jewish families left the life of city apartment-dwellings for the more spacious lawns and gardens of the suburbs. With a little imagination, we may note here a resemblance to an earlier day when the heart of the Jewish community was the synagogue courtyard. To cite one example: in a city like Vilna, which Napoleon called the Jerusalem of Lithuania, the courtyard was the most popular spot for Jews from all walks of life, as well as for visitors in search of friends and clients. Here marriage ceremonies were performed in the open. Here, gathered in one spot, were not only the buildings for worship and study, but also the ritual bath, the ritual slaughterhouse, the administrative offices of the *kehillah* (Jewish community) and the rabbinic courthouse.

The buildings in the suburban communal center of today are different in appearance and atmosphere, reflecting the changed needs and preoccupations of Jews in a far different time and place. Along with the prayer hall and meeting rooms may be found such different facilities as a swimming pool, a kitchen and dining area, a library, museum and an art gallery. Those who belong to a synagogue in this setting may do so for reasons that may be as much social and cultural as religious. Such a synagogue is frankly thought of as a means of counteracting the pressure toward assimilation—a way of keeping the younger generation within the fold of Judaism. Behind the showplace synagogues with their carefully planned facilities is a wish by these relative newcomers to suburban life to have their children feel proud of the faith that is their heritage. The expense of building and maintaining a center of this kind, they reason, is necessary if they are to survive as Jews in the "open" pluralistic society of which they are now a part. The suburban Jewish center is thus often spoken of as the peculiar contribution of American Jewry to the development of the synagogue.

Synagogue Architecture

As we have seen, synagogue architecture through the centuries has tended to reflect the prevailing culture around it. Thus, during the Middle Ages the synagogues of Europe were built in Romanesque or Gothic style, while those in colonial America often borrowed their design from the Protestant churches of the period. As the Jewish newcomers struck roots and became established in the New World, the synagogue boards and architects tended more and more to make the building distinctive by using the symbols of Judaism: the Star of David, the menorah, the Tablets of the Law, the portrayal of a significant Biblical event and the like. In both architecture and decoration, the present-day synagogue expresses a range of possibilities never applied before. An innovative feature is the building arrangement to permit the expansion of seating facilities to accommodate the large numbers of worshipers on the High Holy Days and on special occasions such as graduation and confirmation.

Contemporary synagogue design, both exterior and interior, is a free blend of the old and the new, traditional and experimental, reflecting the varied tastes, origins and conditioning of the congrega-

Sabbath services at the Great Synagogue of Tel Aviv

tional leaders and artists. Some are strongly Hebraic in their outlook; others are "emancipated" and universalistic. In two recent books, *Synagogue Architecture of the United States*, by Rachel Wischnitzer, and *Contemporary Synagogue Art*, by Abraham Kampf, we find numerous striking examples of the work of a number of these artists. The themes they have chosen may be Biblical, legendary, or messianic; the manner may be literal, abstract, or symbolic; the materials may be wood, stone, welded metal, plastic, reinforced concrete, or any other media. It is especially fascinating to see the variety of ways the artists have handled the traditional symbols: the burning bush, the pillar of fire and of cloud, the crown and the Torah scroll, Jacob's ladder, the cherubim, the lion, the tree of life, and so on. One noted artist, Ilia Schor, has specialized in depicting historic events in hammered silver. Another, Raymond Katz, has made decorative use of Hebrew characters in desigining murals and stained-glass windows. Still others, such as Reuben Leaf and Ludwig Wolpert, have used these same characters to develop abstract designs. As in every situation where talented artists have been allowed to experiment with new ideas, people have argued whether the new synagogues are beautiful or bizarre and whether anything so "modern" is proper for a house of worship.

While this question continues to be debated, a more serious one might also be asked: Has all this expenditure of money and talent been for the glory of God or merely for the exaltation of human vanity? Or to put it more pointedly, can Judaism's survival be assured by beautiful buildings alone? Long ago in Talmudic times, Rabbi Mani passing the Great Synagogue of Tiberias uttered the rebuke in Hosea (8:14), *And Israel forgot his master and built temples. Were there no people to study Torah?*, implying that the money could have been used for a better cause. The question is not new. It was asked in another way, we are told, by Rabbi Oshayah in the fourth century when he was shown a splendid new synagogue in Lydda: *Were there no promising scholars who might have been supported by the money spent on this fine building?*

What *shall* be our scale of priorities? Brick and marble or spirit and content? The question is more cogent today than ever. As long as it continues to be asked, there is still hope that the faith out of which the synagogue grew, that has made the institution a living force through centuries of change and of good and bad fortune alike, is still at work today. No institution in the Western world is older than the synagogue. As we pointed out at the beginning of this book, it is so old that scholars disagree on precisely where, when and how it originated. Its establishment was one of the most important landmarks in the history of religion. Churches and mosques followed its pattern. Worship and Torah study took the place of sacrifices. There can, moreover, be no doubt that through the ages, one thing has been at the heart of the synagogue—the identification with, and the devotion of our people to, their most priceless possession, the Law of Moses.

To paraphrase a distinguished Jewish theologian:* We have shown what a unique creation of Judaism the synagogue is. It started on its world mission and made the Torah the common property of the entire people. Established in the Babylonian exile as a substitute for the Temple, it soon eclipsed it as a religious force and a rallying point for the whole people, appealing through the prayers and scriptural lessons to the congregation as a whole. It was not limited to one locality, as the Temple had been, but served and united Jews wherever they settled throughout the world. It eliminated the services of the priest and the sacrificial ritual. It was thus able to spread the truths of Judaism to the remote parts of the earth. It invested the Sabbath and festivals with deeper meaning by utilizing them for instructing and elevating the people spiritually. Study of Torah no less than prayer was propounded as an act of worship and of praise to God. Indeed, the body and the soul of Judaism have lived on indestructibly in the House of Prayer *and* Learning.

Let us end with the fervent prayer: *Ken yehi ratzon*—
May it be God's will; may it ever be so!

*Kaufman Kohler, in *Jewish Theology.*

Torah Pointer (Yad) (18th Century)

Chair of Moses XVII Century-(top left)
Jug for washing hands after burial(center)
Sabbath Lamp—(top right)

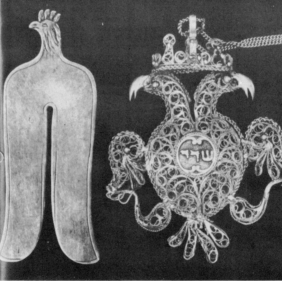

Circumcision clamp and amulet

Torah crown

Menorah

Haman noisemaker

Selected Bibliography

Abrahams, Israel, JEWISH LIFE IN THE MIDDLE AGES, World
  Pub., 1961
Arian, Philip, and Azriel Eisenberg, THE STORY OF THE PRAYER
  BOOK, Prayer Book Press, 1968
Barnett, R., THE SYNAGOGUE OF BEVIS MARKS, Oxford Univ.
  Press, 1960
Baron, Salo W., SOCIAL AND RELIGIOUS HISTORY OF THE
  JEWS, Jewish Publication Society (14 volumes to 1970)
————.THE JEWISH COMMUNITY, (3 volumes) Jewish Publication
  Society, 1942
Blacke, P., AN AMERICAN SYNAGOGUE FOR TODAY AND TO-
  MORROW, Union of American Hebrew Congregations, 1954
COCHIN SYNAGOGUE, 400TH ANNIVERSARY, Cochin, India,
  1968
Cowen, Ida, JEWS IN REMOTE CORNERS OF THE WORLD,
  Prentice Hall, 1971
De Quiros Felipe, T.B., THE SPANISH JEWS (Toledo Synagogues),
  Madrid, 1958 (Brochure)
Eisenberg, Azriel, JEWISH HISTORICAL TREASURES, Bloch Pub.,
  1968
————THE BOOK OF BOOKS, Soncino Press, 1973
FLORENCE SYNAGOGUE, 1958 (Brochure)
Goodenough, Erwin, JEWISH SYMBOLS IN THE GRECO-ROMAN
  WORLD, Pantheon, 1952
Greenbaum, Aaron, THE COCHIN JEWISH COMMUNITY, a re-
  print from *Niv,* Tel Aviv, 1970
Gutfeld, Ludwig, JEWISH ART, Thomas Yoseloff, 1968

Halperin, Don A., THE ANCIENT SYNAGOGUES OF THE IBERIAN PENINSULA, Univ. of Florida Press, 1969

Holisher, Desider, THE SYNAGOGUE AND ITS PEOPLE, Abelard-Schuman, 1955

Katz, Raymond A., A NEW ART FOR AN OLD RELIGION, Russel F. Moore Co., 1952

Kampf, Avram, CONTEMPORARY SYNAGOGUE ART, Union of American Hebrew Congregations, 1966

Kayser, Stephen S. JEWISH CEREMONIAL AND RITUAL ART, Jewish Publication Society, 1955

Kline, Alexander, S., and others, CONTEMPORARY DEVELOPMENT IN AMERICAN SYNAGOGUE ART, Union of American Hebrew Congregations

Kohler, Kaufman, THE ORIGINS OF THE SYNAGOGUE AND THE CHURCH, Macmillan, 1929

Kon, Abraham, PRAYER, London, Soncino Press, 1972

Kraeling, C.H., THE EXCAVATION OF DURA-EUROPOS: THE SYNAGOGUE, Yale Univ. Press, 1956

Landman, Leo, THE CANTOR: A HISTORIC PERSPECTIVE, Yeshiva University, 1972

Landsberger, F.A., HISTORY OF JEWISH ART, Union of Amercian Hebrew Congregations, 1946

Loukomiski, George, JEWISH ART EUROPEAN SYNAGOGUES, London, Hutchinson, 1947

Levy, Isaac, THE SYNAGOGUE: ITS HISTORY AND FUNCTION, London, Valentine Mitchell, 1966

Martin, Bernard, PRAYER IN JUDAISM, Basic Books, 1968

Millgram, Abraham E., JEWISH WORSHIP, Jewish Publication Society 1971

Mitten, David Gordon, THE ANCIENT SYNAGOGUE OF SARDIS (brochure), Committee on Synagogue of Sardis, Cambridge, Mass., Harvard Univ. Press

Morris, Nathan, THE JEWISH SCHOOL: An Introduction to the History of Jewish Education, New York, Jewish Education Committee Press, 1937

Newman, J., SEMIKHA (Ordination), Manchester University, England, 1950

Newman, Louis I., MAGGIDIM, HASIDIM: THEIR WISDOM, Bloch
    Pub., 1962

Postal, Bernard, and S. Abrahamson, LANDMARKS OF A PEOPLE,
    Hill and Wang, 1962

Piechotka, Maria, and Kazimierz, WOODEN SYNAGOGUES, Ar-
    kady, 1956

Roth, Cecil, (ed.), JEWISH ART, McGraw-Hill, 1961: Synagogue Ar-
    chitecture by Aharon Kashtan, pp 253–308; Ritual Art by Cecil
    Roth, pp 309–350.

Roth, Cecil, JEWISH ART, AN ILLUSTRATED HISTORY, McGraw
    Hill, 1961

Sassoon, David Solomon, A HISTORY OF THE JEWS IN BAGH-
    DAD, Letchworth, England, 1949

Squarciapino, M. Floriani, SYNAGOGUE OF OSTIA, Rome, 1964
    (Brochure)

Sukenik, Eliezer, ANCIENT SYNAGOGUES OF PALESTINE AND
    GREECE, London, 1934

THE PINKAS SYNAGOGUE, Prague, 1955

THE STATE JEWISH MUSEUM IN PRAGUE, n. d.

Volakova, Hanna, THE SYNAGOGUE TREASURES OF BOHEMIA
    AND MORAVIA, Prague, 1949

Wischnitzer, Rachel, THE ARCHITECTURE OF THE EUROPEAN
    SYNAGOGUE, Jewish Publication Society, 1964

SYNAGOGUE ARCHITECTURE IN THE UNITED STATES, Jew-
    ish Publication Society, 1955

THE MESSIANIC THEME IN THE PAINTINGS OF THE DURA
    SYNAGOGUE, Univ. of Chicago Press, 1948

Holy Ark and Bimah (eighteenth century) from Padua, now in Heichal Shlomo, Jerusalem

*Old Torah Scroll and ornaments
in the Italian Synagogue, Jerusalem*

*Seventeenth-century brass Hanukkah
Candelabrum now in Italian Synagogue*

Index

S. stands for synagogue(s)
fn. stands for footnote